MARINA TSVETAYEVA
SELECTED POEMS

Selected Poems

Marina Tsvetayeva

BLOODAXE BOOKS

ISBN: 1 85224 025 3

First published 1987 by
Bloodaxe Books Ltd,
P.O. Box 1SN,
Newcastle upon Tyne NE99 1SN.

Bloodaxe Books Ltd acknowledges
the financial assistance of Northern Arts.

ACKNOWLEDGEMENTS
The introductory essay and several of the translations from this book were first published in *Parnassus*. F.F. Morton's versions first appeared in the *New Yorker*.
Thanks are due to Liza Knapp of Columbia University for her editorial advice.

Cover illustration by Michael Caine

Typesetting by Bryan Williamson, Manchester.

Printed in Great Britain by
Bell & Bain Limited, Glasgow, Scotland.

Contents

FROM POEMS OF YOUTH (1913-18)

35 This gypsy passion
36 With great tenderness
37 You that make your way
38 For my poems
39 Some forebear of mine
40 Much like me
41 Every poem is a child of love
42 I'm happy to live like a paragon
43 Bring me what others don't require
44 My horse

FROM BON-VOYAGES (1921-22)

47 I bless the daily labour
48 *From* Bon-Voyages
49 Make merry, my soul
50 God stooped
51 *From* Insomnia
52 No one has taken away anything
53 *From the cycle* Poems to Akhmatova

FROM SWANS' ENCAMPMENT: POEMS 1917-1921

56 From the church so austere and shapely
57 *From* André Chénier
58 Wretched are the strong and wealthy
59 We must declare ourselves boldly, lyre
60 White is a threat to Blackness's field
61 Night. Nor'-easter
62 White Guards
63 All this is simple as blood and sweat are
64 As you fought for your fatherland
65 If the soul was born with pinions
66 Above the churchtower there are clouds of blue

FROM THE CRAFT (1923)

68 *From* Girlhood
70 *From* The Disciple

FROM AFTER RUSSIA: POEMS 1922-1925

72 In Praise of the Rich
74 Grey Hairs
75 *From* The Poet
77 The Hour of the Soul
80 Deuce
83 The Demon in Me
84 Beware
86 The Window

UNCOLLECTED POEMS

89 I will win you away from every earth
90 Nailed against the shameful stake
91 Bush
93 Table
97 I've dissolved for you
98 House
100 United as the left hand and the right
101 Looking for the motherland
103 Elder
105 My window
106 I used to write it out on schoolroom slates
107 Poems grow
108 My day
109 There are happy men and women
110 You, who love me
111 Garden
112 I'm a sheet of paper for your pen
113 I thank you, Lord
114 I've opened my veins
115 Poem of the End
140 Poems to Czechia
148 An Attempt at a Room
155 New Year Letter

Introduction

Idealism, particularly idealism of a cultural or artistic kind, has become such a rare phenomenon in the contemporary world that it may often be hard for us to feel our way into the spiritual background of much of the art, music, and literature that burst upon an unsuspecting European public in the last years of the 19th century and the early years of the 20th. It has become fashionable to suppose that what we have come to term variously "modern art", "modern music", or simply "modernism" took its origins in some collective artistic rejection of the styles and norms of the past, and in an adoption of a sceptical and anti-idealistic world view. While it is true that the "iconoclastic" movements of expressionism, futurism, dada, and early surrealism relied for much of their public impact on shock-tactics and a philosophy of 'making it new', a close study of their artistic programmes shows that their primary concern was less the destruction of the past than the reinterpretation of both past and present in terms of a visionary future, a hoped-for world in which the artist, like some divinely inspired child, would endow mankind with a new innocence, exorcising from it the demons of war, revolution, technology, and social organisation. Such a transformed humanity would be a worthy successor to the mankind of previous ages – the artist would simply have acted as a necessary catalyst to further growth, a spiritual yeast and ferment in a dangerously god-deprived world. This quest was, of course, profoundly idealistic, and it was by no means confined to the artistic programmes of any particular school. The school-transcending work of Mahler, Scriabin, Schoenberg, and Stravinsky, of Kandinsky and Malevich, of George and Rilke – all of them in some sense deeply religious artists – might be seen as an attempt to write a gospel for the age, to effect by tonal, visual, and verbal means a ritual sacrifice (the artist as saviour) and subsequent transfiguration of the human soul at an absolute level.

Nowhere was this metaphysical, artistic striving so evident as in Russia in the late years of the last century and the early years of the present one. Perhaps the onset of the 20th century, in which the metaphor of the artist as saviour was in Russia, at any rate, to acquire a thoroughly real and non-metaphoric (though nonetheless symbolic) double in the form of its finest poets' destinies, was felt particularly keenly in a country where the potential for disaster of all kinds was so great. Mention of Scriabin, Stravinsky, and Kandinsky leads us inevitably to a long list of the names of artists, poets, and composers for whom the process of creation was by no means confined to the production of individual works, or even linked to any one art in particular, but was rather a path towards the infinite and towards an ultimate revelation of the soul. Boris Pasternak describes, in his autobiographical essay 'Safe Conduct', the tortuous path by which he found his way from a semi-mystical identification with the music of Scriabin, through an attempt, in Marburg, to assimilate the essence of German neo-Kantian thought, to the realisation that he was, in fact, a poet. Such cosmic and cultural pilgrimages were certainly not rare among literary artists in the Russia of the pre-Revolutionary years. Marina Tsvetayeva, who was born two years later than Pasternak, in 1892, and who like him grew up in a musical-artistic Moscow family, was exposed early on to the most diverse cultural influences. Her father was a well-known philologist and art critic, a professor at the University of Moscow who also founded the Moscow Museum of Fine Arts (now known as the Pushkin Museum of Visual Arts). Her mother, who came of Russified Polish-German stock, was a musician, a pupil of Anton Rubinstein; her dream had been to become a concert pianist, but her father had not approved of this ambition – she had obeyed his wishes, and had instead brought up a family of children. Tsvetayeva wrote later that she owed her mother 'everything': 'Music, nature, poetry, Germany ...One against all. Heroica.' When Tsvetayeva was only 14, her mother died; her father died when she was 21.

The significance of Tsvetayeva's intense and closely delineated childhood for her later development as a poet is quite evident from even the most cursory glance at the events of her biography. Her mother's unsatisfied longings for artistic achievement, linked with a perpetual striving for the heroic and the exalted, must have had a profound influence on her daughters Marina and Ariadna. In Marina's case, this unfulfilled pianism had the effect of alienating her from the practice of music-making: instead of playing the piano, she shut herself up in her room and wrote poetry. This started at a very early age, and it tended to isolate her quite considerably from the rest of the family. Alone in her room, Marina composed poems which reflected the multilingual education given her by her mother: when she was unable to find a Russian rhyme for a word, she would insert a German or a French word that did rhyme. Meanwhile the house would be filled with the din of piano music.

In 1902, when Tsvetayeva was ten, her mother contracted tuberculosis and had to go abroad in search of treatment. She took Marina and Ariadna with her on these journeys, to Italy, France, Switzerland,

and Germany. While the mother was treated at spas and clinics, the daughters received instruction at local boarding schools. French and German became just as familiar to them as Russian – so much so that their father was afraid they might forget their native language altogether, and packed Russian books along with the slabs of black bread he was fond of sending. The experience of foreign countries and this semi-independent life away from her mother were strong factors in Tsvetayeva's self-discovery as a poet. The sporadic, unstable nature of her education may also have been in part responsible for her later difficulty in finding an "accepted" place in society.

After the death of her mother in 1906, Marina went to school in Moscow. Much of the time, however, she played truant. Music was no longer the influence it had been – Marina was free to devote herself to her own interests: a cult of Napoleon and his son (an extreme manifestation of a form of hero-worship relatively common among young Russian girls who had read *War and Peace*) and poetry. It is important to bear in mind that throughout the years of Tsvetayeva's childhood and adolescence the great flowering of Russian symbolism was taking place. These were the years of Bryusov's largely successful adaptation of western (mostly French) verse experiments into Russian linguistic and cultural terms, of the emergence of Aleksandr Blok with his 'Beautiful Lady', and of the strange, anthroposophy- and demon-obsessed Andrey Bely, whose cosmically storm-ridden poetry still awaits translation into English. That Tsvetayeva was deeply influenced by Bely's work and spirit is beyond doubt[1] – her memoir *Captive Spirit*, written in Paris after Bely's death in 1934, describes the lifelong debt she felt she owed her 'white angel', whose mysterious name (a pseudonym, meaning, 'Andrew the White' – his real name was Boris Aleksandrovich Bugayev), entering into her childhood for the first time on the lips of her scandalised Aunt Yelizaveta, came to occupy a central significance in her life. Marina experienced Symbolism less as an artistic theory or programme than as the sum of certain very powerful contemporary poetic personalities – they included Blok, Vyacheslav Ivanov, and Bely himself, of whom she wrote, remembering her earliest living encounters with him in the year 1910:

> ...I often used to see him...in Musaget,[2] but saw him, rather than talked to him; most often his back would be turned to me, as he danced to and fro with a stick of white chalk in his hand in front of the blackboard, which would instantly be peppered – it was as if they flew out of his coatsleeves! – with the commas, half-moons and zigzags of rhythmic schemes, which I found so reminiscent of our geometry lessons at school

that I found myself yielding to a perfectly natural instinct for self-preservation (what if he were to suddenly turn round and call me out to the blackboard?) and letting my attention stray from Bely's dancing back to the immobile faces of Staatsrat Goethe and Dr Steiner who stared at us from the wall with enormous eyes that were perhaps, come to think of it, not staring at us at all.

That is still how I remember him: the early Bely dancing before Goethe and Steiner, as once David danced before the ark of the covenant. In the life of a symbolist everything is a symbol. There is nothing that is not symbolic.

It might with some justice be said that Tsvetayeva developed the philosophy and aesthetics of symbolism to their ultimate limits. It certainly became true of her own life that 'everything is a symbol' – a symbol of the poet's own fate as an outcast, and of the counterweight she placed against it, that of an all-inclusive love.

Marina's cult of Napoleon was as ardent as her veneration of Bely. She read everything that had been written about Napoleon and his son – her bedroom at home was festooned with portraits of them, and she would lock herself away for long hours in her 'Napoleon studies'. In the summer of 1909, when she was seventeen, she went to Paris, where she visited all the relics of Napoleon she could find, and began to translate Rostand's *L'Aiglon*. At the same time she took an informal course in Old French literature at the Sorbonne.

In 1910, the year of the Bely lectures, appeared the eighteen-year-old Tsvetayeva's first book of poems, *Vecherniy Al'bom* (Evening Album):

Having a book published was a simple matter in those days: you simply got your poems together, took them down to a printer's, selected a binding, paid your money, and there you were. And that's what I did, without telling anyone about it beforehand, a sixth-form schoolgirl. After the copies had been printed, I took all 500 of them down to the godforsaken bookshop of Spiridonov & Mikhailov, who stored them away in their warehouse... and then I breathed a sigh of relief.

The poems of this first and quite extensive collection (it contains some 111 lyrics), which have only recently become available again in the five-volume Russian-language *Collected Poems* published by Russica in New York, may come as a surprise to a reader acquainted only with the work of Tsvetayeva's maturity. There are few – one might even say no – signs of Bely's influence, and the prevailing impression is of a neat, orderly arrangement of regularly rhyming stanzas. The rhymes are by and large conventional although, as pointed out earlier, there are occasional bilingual rhymes *(dushi-Ouchy, Kavaler-Herr)*, and a mild tendency toward assonantal rhyming.

Many of the poems depict domestic scenes and incidents: the poet's mother reading Lichtenstein to her daughters; the German governess looking out of the window at a blind organ-grinder, weeping as the music reminds her of her own personal loss and endeavouring to hide her tears from the children in her care; a necklace of green stones that breaks, involving the sisters in a hunt for the 'chrysolites' of life, 'not glass fakes'; the poet's depression during the interval of twilight between four and seven in the evening; the death of her mother. The presence – and deeply grieved absence – of the mother is a constant theme in the poems. Bryusov, reviewing the volume, found it impressive ('Reading her book, one occasionally grows uneasy, for it is as if one had indiscreetly looked through a half-open window into someone else's apartment and seen something one was not supposed to'); but this effect is rather overdone at times, and occasionally borders on monotony. There is evidence of a reading of George and Rilke (particularly the *Neue Gedichte*, which had appeared in 1907) and possibly also of Verlaine. The studies of interiors, of afternoons in childhood, memories of Paris and Berlin flow together in an undifferentiated fashion, and one has the sense that the collection's significance lies less in its contents and subject matter than in its stylistic characteristics, in particular its bold and imaginative use of language and languages to create a fresh, spontaneous verse texture. It may be possible to give the reader of English an impression of the slightly breathless, dashing, and cosmopolitan flavour of the volume by quoting a few isolated lines and stanzas at random:

Drozhat na lyustrakh ogon'ki....
Kak khorosho za knigoy doma!
Pod Griga, Shumana i Kyui
Ya uznavala sud'by Toma....

The lights are trembling on the chandeliers....
How good to be at home with a book!
To the strains of Grieg, Schumann and Cui
I learned the fate of Tom....
('Books in Red Bindings')

Fräulein plachet: volnuyet igra!
Vodit mal'chik perom po b'yuvaru.
– 'Ne grusti, lieber Junge, – pora
Nam gulyat' po Tverskomu bul'varu.

The Fräulein weeps: the playing agitates her!
The boy trails his pen across the blotting paper.

'Don't be sad, lieber Junge, – it's time
For us to take our walk along Tver' Boulevard....
('Street Organ in Spring')

'Plyvite!' molvila Vesna.
Ushla zemlya, sverknula pena,
Divan-korabl' v ozyorakh sna
Pomchal nas k skazke Andersena.

'Set sail!' said Spring.
The land receded, the foam sparkled,
On lakes of sleep the sofa-ship
Carried us off to a fairytale by Andersen....
('First Voyage')

The collection is dedicated 'to the glorious memory of Maria Bashkirtseva' (a Russian woman painter whose diary was the favourite reading of many generations of romantically-inclined young girls), and contains numerous epigraphs in the form of quotations from Edmond Rostand *('Ah, mieux vaut repartir aussitôt qu'on arrive / Que de te voir faner, nouveauté de la rive')*, from the First Epistle of John ('There is no fear in love; but perfect love casteth out fear: because fear hath torment. He that feareth is not perfect in love.') and Napoleon I *('L'imagination gouverne le monde')*, among others. Tsvetayeva later wrote that she published her *Evening Album* 'instead of writing letters to someone with whom it would not otherwise have been possible for me to communicate'.

In addition to the notice by Bryusov alluded to earlier, the book received favourable reviews from a number of other poet-critics, including Nikolay Gumilyov, and Maksimilian Voloshin, who wrote:

> The book is poised on the borderline that separates the last days of childhood from the first days of young adulthood. If one adds that not only does its author possess a master of verse-writing, but also a faculty for inner observation in terms of a clearly-focused exterior, an impressionistic ability to transfix the fleeting moment, one gains a clear awareness of the documentary significance of this book, which concerns those years in which the verbal facility is as yet insufficiently developed to allow the faithful expression of observations and emotions.

Voloshin, a well-known painter and poet, was at the centre of a literary and artistic "bohemian" circle which had its base in the Black Sea coastal town of Koktebel'. Voloshin's favourable review led to Tsvetayeva becoming acquainted with this bearded, peasant-clad guru, and to her spending a good deal of time among his entourage in Koktebel'. It was here that Voloshin prophesied all the events of the Russian revolution and Civil War. Viktoria Schweitzer, the noted Russian émigré authority on Tsvetayeva's biography and writings, has described the Koktebel' community in the following terms: 'Here inspiration was born. It seemed that here one could be alone with the elements: Fire, the Sun which heated the earth so much that it cracked, and burned one's feet through one's light summer shoes; the element of Earth, which seemed as if only recently arisen out of chaos, still primordial in its wrinkled unadornedness. The element of Water, of the sea, surging and receding, like a living creature, something that constantly spoke in its own language, forgotten by human beings':

> ...and now Homer is silent,
> And the Black Sea roars its oratory
> And lunges at the bedpost with lugubrious din.
>
> (Osip Mandelstam)[3]

In Koktebel' the circle of painters, actors, writers, and poets lived a life apart, a life of union with nature, of 'friendship, freedom, and lack of inhibition'. In the daytime they worked in their studios, or went for long walks alone in the hills – at night they would gather in Voloshin's studio and read poetry aloud to one another, or stroll along the beach in the moonlight. It was in this artistic environment that Tsvetayeva met her future husband, Sergey Efron. They fell in love instantly – she was 19 years old, he 18. Tsvetayeva blossomed out. For a long time she had considered herself plain and unattractive. Schweitzer writes: 'She had possessed in her own view a rather prosaic appearance: she was round-faced and rosy-cheeked. By the time she was 20 she had lost weight, grown slender, passionate, and she herself now noticed her luxuriant golden hair and her green eyes the colour of gooseberries....'

Tsvetayeva and Efron married in January, 1912, the year which also saw the publication of Tsvetayeva's second book of poems, *Volshebnyy fonar'* – 'Magic Lantern'. This represented a continuation of the themes and style of *Evening Album*, but was less successful with the critics. Later, in retrospect, Tsvetayeva claimed that *Evening Album* and *Magic Lantern* 'were really one book'. In January 1913, the couple had their first child, their daughter Ariadna. This was the happiest period of Tsvetayeva's life. She spent much of the time in Koktebel', but also travelled to Theodosia and Moscow. In Moscow she discovered a circle of young student actors who read and admired her poems. One of the students described Tsvetayeva thus:

> ....She lowered her hood and I saw her luxuriant cap of golden hair. I stood behind her and Oh! what a dress she was wearing! It was unusual, ravishing: silken, browny-gold, wide, flowing luxuriantly down to the floor, the narrow waist firmly gathered in by an old-fashioned corsage. At the slightly open neck, a precious stone. A magical girl from the last century! She walked past, and I noticed that she was not alone. Her companion – a young man – never took his eyes off his lady. I went to one side to get a clothes-hanger, and found myself involuntarily observing him (he did not see me): he was tall, thin, slightly stooping. His head had a noble outline, his thick, black hair was smoothed combed and parted in the middle. In his large, grey-blue eyes there occasionally flared a boyish, impudent, but sensitive humour....I couldn't stop watching Marina Tsvetayeva. Under the cap of her golden hair I could see the oval of her face, broad on top, tapering below, her fine nose with its barely imperceptible aquiline trait, and her greenish eyes, the eyes of an enchantress.

Tsvetayeva loved the Crimea – its sun, wind, evenings with crackling fires. Her adolescent crush on Napoleon was forgotten: from now on her poems were peopled by real human beings, and she took an increasingly acute interest in the psychology of love relationships, in shades of feelings and thought. Although some poems of this period centre on a romantically idealised image of Efron, others, notably the long cycle *Podruga* (The Girl Friend), addressed to Sofia Parnok, conjure up a living woman, though an adored one:

My byli: ya – v pyshnom plat'e
Iz chut' zolotogo faya,
Vy – v vyazanoy chornoy kurtke
S krylatym vorotnikom.

Ya pomnyu, s kakim voshli Vy
Litsom – bez maleyshey kraski,
Kak vstali, kusaya pal'chik,
Chut' golovu naklonya.

I lob Vash vlastolyubivyy
Pod tyazhest'yu ryzhey kaski,
Ne zhenshchina i ne mal'chik, –
No chto-to sil'ney menya!

I was wearing a magnificent dress
Of slightly golden poult-de-soie,
You had on a black knitted jacket
With a winged collar.

I remember your face when you
Came in – it had not the slightest colour,
How you rose, biting your finger,
Your head slightly inclined.

And your forehead, aspiring to power,
Beneath the weight of its chestnut helmet,
Not a woman and not a boy,
But somehow stronger than I.

At the same time the diction of her poems grew sharper and more disciplined, their tone more adult and mature. Eventually, she gathered the poems written during this time under the title *Yunoshes-kiye stikhi* (Poems of Youth), a collection which was never published in her lifetime, but which marked her artistic breakthrough. In these poems we can at last see the fruits of Tsvetayeva's contact with the poetry of symbolism, in particular with the springing rhythms and dashes of Bely's verse, and the grave, passionate recklessness of Blok's. The poems are a challenge and a testament:

Idyosh', na menya pokhozhiy,
Glaza ustremlyaya vniz.
Ya ikh opuskala – tozhe!
Prokhozhiy, ostanovis'!

Prochti – slepoty kurinoy
I makov nabrav buket –
Chto zvali menya Marinoy
I skol'ko mne bylo let.

Ne dumay, chto zdes' – mogila,
Chto ya poyavlyus', grozya…
Ya slishkom sama lyubila
Smeyat'sya, kogda nel'zya!

I krov' prilivala k kozhe,
I kudri moi vilis'…
Ya tozhe byla, *prokhozhiy!*
Prokhozhiy, ostanovis'!

Much like me, you make your way forward,
Walking with downturned eyes.
Well, I too kept mine lowered.
Passer-by, stop here, please.

Read, when you've picked your nosegay
Of henbane and poppy flowers,
That I was once called Marina,
And discover how old I was.

Don't think that there's any grave here,
Or that I'll come and throw you out….
I myself was too much given
To laughing when one ought not.

The blood hurtled to my complexion,
My curls wound in flourishes....
I *was*, passer-by, I existed!
Passer-by, stop here, please....

This was the time of her friendship with the young Osip Mandelstam. The two poets met in St Petersburg during the winter of 1915-16. Later, Mandelstam came to Moscow, where Tsvetayeva 'made a gift of Moscow to him':

Iz ruk moikh – nerukotvornyy grad
Primi, moy strannyy, moy prekrasny brat...

Take from my hands this city built not by hands,
My strange, my beautiful brother...

Viktoria Schweitzer writes:

> That summer he stayed with her in Aleksandrovo, near Moscow: Tsvetayeva revealed to him, the European and St Petersburger, another Russia – an Oriental, wooden, Muscovite one...So frequently did Mandelstam visit Moscow during those months that friends used to say jokingly: 'I wonder if he's working on the railway?' He even thought of moving to Moscow and trying to get a job (!) there...Mandelstam's first poems of 1916 are Muscovite, "Tsvetayevan" ones.

In the end, though, in Tsvetayeva's words, Mandelstam 'ran away' from her, intimidated perhaps by her 'insatiability', with which she 'overfed' everyone (Tsvetayeva's own words).

Tsyganskaya strast' razluki!
Chut' vstretish' – uzh rvyosh'sya proch'!
Ya lob uronila v ruki,
I dumayu, glyadya v noch':

Nikto, v nashikh pis'makh royas',
Ne ponyal do glubiny,
Kak my verolomny, to yest' –
Kak sami sebe verny.

This gypsy passion for parting!
We just meet, yet already take flight!
My brow's in my hands, I'm starting
To think, looking out through the night

That those who ransack our letters
Have only perceived by halves
How faithless we are, and that is –
How faithful we are to ourselves.

The volume includes a poem to Akhmatova (it was to be followed, in *Vyorsty*, by a whole cycle of remarkable poems dedicated to her). Although Tsvetayeva admired and revered Akhmatova as a poet for most of her creative life, the two women were never close, and indeed did not meet one another until the winter of 1939-40, after Tsvetayeva's return to the Soviet Union.

There are poems to Efron:

Ya s vyzovom noshu ego kol'tso
– Da, v Vechnosti – zhena, ne na bumage –
Yego chrezmerno uzkoye litso
Podobno shpage....

It's with defiance that I wear his ring
– Yes, in Eternity a wife, and not on paper –
His face, so narrow and so thin
Is like a sabre....

Again, Tsvetayeva takes up childhood memories – of life with her sister, of Germany. But now a note of genuine passion creeps into her voice, as personally experienced time begins to unite with history:

Ty miru otdana na travlyu,
I schota net tvoim vragam.
Nu, kak zhe ya *tebya ostavlyu.*
Nu, kak zhe ya *tebe predam.*

You've been abandoned to the world's taunts
Your enemies are numberless.
Well, how could *I* ever leave you?
Well, how could *I* ever betray you?
('To Germany')

The passion in those italicised 'I''s was a response to real historical events, which tore at the fabric of individual life. The turbulence of the First World War were a brutal termination to the Koktebel' idyll. In 1914 Efron volunteered for the front. By 1917 he was an officer, stationed in Moscow with the 56th Reserve Regiment. Tsvetayeva was afraid for his health – he had tuberculosis. During the war years, she lived in Moscow, but in the summer of 1917 she contemplated moving to Theodosia, away from the famine that had developed in Moscow. She dreamed that Efron might be able to obtain leave and join her in the south, but this was not to be. Her children now in care, Tsvetayeva went to Theodosia alone at the beginning of October, to try to find somewhere for herself and her family to live. While she was there, she saw some of the results of the February revolution. The populace had raided the town's municipal wine cellars, and the streets flowed, quite literally, with wine. 'Even the birds were drunk,' the poet recalled some years later.

Tsvetayeva witnessed the October revolution directly, at first hand, in the train journeys she made between Moscow and Theodosia throughout the autumn. In the trains she came into contact with the ordinary Russian people for the first time, and was shocked by the violence and ugliness of the atmosphere. 'In the air of the compartment there hung only three axe-like words: *bourgeois, Junkers, bloodsuckers*,' she wrote in her diary. 'People, people, people. Fear, hatred, stupidity, baseness... Foul language...' At last it became impossible to travel to the Crimea any more – Russia had, in fulfilment of one of Voloshin's prophecies, become divided into two countries: North and South.

Efron went off to fight as a White Guard, and Tsvetayeva was left alone in Moscow, in conditions of extreme poverty and hardship. She was now 25 years old, and she had two children, Ariadna and Irina, to look after. Somehow she managed to scrape a living together from odd jobs in libraries and bakeries. Most of the time she and her family went hungry – Tsvetayeva lived largely on the charity of friends and neighbours, and she even stole in her attempts to feed her children. She described everything she experienced and saw during this time, and recorded it in the book that was eventually titled *Earthly Traits (Zemnyye primety)*. One of these notes reads: "I won't leave you." Only God can say such a thing – or a peasant with milk in Moscow during the winter of 1918.'

It was not until 1921 that Tsvetayeva was able to organise, edit, and arrange as collections the poems she had written during these years of appalling hardship and suffering. The first two of these collections bear the title *Vyorsty* (literally, 'versts', the old Russian measure of distance). The third, *Lebedinyy stan* (the nearest English translation is 'Swans' Encampment'), remained unpublished until long after her death (it was published in 1957 by a firm in Munich). While the poems of the *Vyorsty* collections represent, by and large, a continuation and development of Tsvetayeva's previously published collections (the first poem in *Vyorsty I* is dated January 1916, and seems to take up where the last poem of *Yunosheskiye stikhi* left off), those of *Lebedinyy stan* possess a radically different tonality. This poetry of the immediate post-revolutionary time is stark, denuded of ornament, directly personal, and yet also addressed to the age and its evil. There is no mistaking where the poet's sympathies lie:

Belogvardeytsy! Gordyy uzel
Doblesti russkoy!
Belogvardeytsy! Belyye gruzdi
Pesenki russkoy!
Belogvardeytsy! Belyye zvyozdy!
S neba ne vyskresti!
Belogvardeytsy! Chornyye gvozdi
V rebra Antikhristu!

White Guards: Gordian knot
Of Russian valour.
White Guards: white mushrooms
Of the Russian folksong.
White Guards: white stars,
Not to be crossed from the sky.
White Guards: black nails
In the ribs of the Antichrist.

Soviet literary critics are still fond of claiming that Tsvetayeva 'neither accepted nor understood' the Bolshevik revolution. The truth is, however, that while she did not accept the revolution, she understood it only too well, and was deeply, personally repelled by what she saw and witnessed:

– Svoboda! – Gulyashchaya devka
Na shaloy soldatskoy grudi!

Freedom – a drunken whore sprawling
In a power-maddened soldier's arms.

('From the stern and shapely temple')

Yet it would be a mistake to view Tsvetayeva's position at this time as being one of a narrow political alignment. Schweitzer writes:

In these poems we are struck not only by the good-naturedness, the readiness to forgive, but also by the faithfulness and sobriety of the poet's gaze, and by the precision of the words with which she described the participation in the Civil War of the 'little ones' – the ordinary Russian people. Like a mother, Tsvetayeva mourns for all those who have died in the fratricidal war – both Whites and Reds.

As an instance of this attitude, we might quote from one of the poems in *Lebedinyy stan* which expresses her new world-outlook:

I have two enemies in all the world,
Two twins, inseparably pooled:
The hunger of the hungry and the fullness of the full.

('If the soul was born with pinions')

Schweitzer tells us that Tsvetayeva changed outwardly during this period of her life. 'She lost her rosy cheeks, and there appeared instead an earthy-swarthy facial colour which was to stay with her for the rest of her life. She grew thinner.'

Ariadna was Tsvetayeva's principal friend and helper during this period. Ariadna (or Alya) was only five years old at the time the revolution began – yet she helped her mother, knew all her mother's friends, and even kept diaries of the life she had led with her.[4] The diary-keeping also had an educational purpose – this was Marina's method of teaching her daughter to read and write.

Tsvetayeva's younger daughter, Irina, was less fortunate: weak and sickly, she developed slowly and poorly, and could hardly walk by the time she was three. The years of privation and hunger had their effect: in 1920 Irina died of malnutrition in the orphanage where Tsvetayeva had been compelled to leave her.

Tsvetayeva did not see Efron from 1917 until 1922, and did not know whether he was alive or not. In 1921 the poet and critic Il'ya Ehrenburg tracked him down in Czechoslovakia. In 1922 Tsvetayeva left Moscow with Ariadna, and together they went to Berlin, where Efron had moved.

The time in Berlin was something of a transitional stage for Efron and Tsvetayeva. They made many contacts among the émigré intelligentsia: Tsvetayeva formed a short-lived relationship with Bely – at last she was able to meet and talk with the poet she had so long admired. The poems that Tsvetayeva wrote in Berlin are written in a classical and austere style, which found its clearest and finest expression in the collection *The Craft (Remeslo)*, published in 1923. No translation can ever really hope to capture the distinctive essence of these poems, which possess a peculiarly "Russo-European" quality, akin to that found in the neo-classical compositions of Stravinsky that date from the same period, and in some of the Berlin and Paris painting of the Russian artists of the time, such as Kandinsky, Malevich and Goncharova. This was the period before Russia and the West became completely cut off from one another, and there was still a good deal of movement between Berlin and Paris, then the artistic capitals of Europe, and the cities of Leningrad and Moscow. The poems of *Remeslo* reflect the artistic and cultural ferment of the time, and indeed they are the nearest thing to "modern" poems in the whole of Tsvetayeva's poetic output which, like that of Akhmatova and Mandelstam, is essentially conservative in aesthetic and formal terms. Some of the poems also clearly show the influence of Bely – the abundant use of the dash, and the heavily-marked rhythms derive from him, rather than from Mayakovsky, as is sometimes suggested. Other poems are more restrained in formal terms, yet radiate an intense charge of emotion which at times threatens to break out violently:

Tý v nochi nachosivala grebnem,
Tý v nochi ottachivala strely.
Shchedrost'yu tvoyey davyas', kak shchebnem,
Za chuzhie ya grekhi terpela.

Skipetr tebe vernula do sroku –
Chtó uzhe dushe do yastv i brashna!
Molodos' moya! Moya moroka –
Molodos'! Moy loskutok kumashnyy!

At nights *you* scoured me with your carding comb,
At nights *you* sharpened your arrows.
Choked on *your* gifts as on a chip of stone,
I paid not for my sins, but someone else's.

I hand your sceptre back before it's time.
What, to the soul, are food and being full?
My girlhood! Mischief-maker, dark and gloom –
My girlhood! You, my red rag to the bull!
('My Girlhood')

Tsvetayeva and Efron seem to have decided that a Slavic milieu would be more congenial to them, for in 1923 they moved to Czechoslovakia. They were unable to find living accommodation that they could afford in Prague itself. Efron, studying politics and sociology at Prague University, lived in a series of student hostels, while Tsvetayeva and Ariadna found rooms in villages outside town. Tsvetayeva and her husband spent only one winter, that of 1923-24, together in Prague itself – during this time, Ariadna was in boarding school. The family's only real "income" was Efron's student grant, which was eked out by Tsvetayeva's "allowance" from the Czech government (a small pension paid to immigrants from Russia – scholars and writers). Tsvetayeva and Efron were among the least well-off in the emigration – they had lost everything in the revolution, and now their life was in many ways not much easier than it had been in Moscow. There were the same depressing concerns about getting enough food, drawing water from the well, gathering firewood in mud up to the knee. On top of all this, Efron's health began to deteriorate. He contracted tuberculosis, and for the rest of his life he was a semi-invalid. This was an additional burden on the family, as it meant that he was unable to work at anything except his political activity and sociological studies. To outsiders, it often seemed as though Marina had been left with only the shell of a husband – the burnt-out reality of the romantic knight in shining armour she had once adored and sung of in her poems. Yet Tsvetayeva continued to be loyal to Efron right up to the end, even after his disappearance in 1937 and evident involvement with the Soviet secret police.

On the other hand, Tsvetayeva did manage to form some important personal contacts in Czechoslovakia. Above all, she befriended Anna Antonovna Teskovà, a woman who had spent her childhood years in Russia, and who spoke excellent Russian. Teskovà, who was some twenty years older that Tsvetayeva, was a writer and the director of the Czechoslovak-Russian 'Union' *(Česko-ruská Jednota)*, and she introduced Tsvetayeva to university circles in Prague; her personal warmth and motherly solicitude transmitted itself through her letters. Teskovà and Tsvetayeva did not meet frequently, but the correspondence they began in these years continued right up until Tsvetayeva's departure for the Soviet Union. It was an important moral and psychological support for the poet, and it helped her through some of the most agonising moments of the difficult years of the life she had left to live.

In Prague Tsvetayeva also befriended Boris Pasternak, with whom she began a correspondence that lasted until her return to Russia, and was another important source of moral and spiritual support for her. Although Tsvetayeva loved Pasternak, and he was for a long time deeply attached to her, there was never any question of their living together. Tsvetayeva remained with Efron, and most of her relations with Pasternak, as with other male companions, were conducted in epistolary form.

Another important event at this time was the birth of Tsvetayeva's son Georgiy (or 'Mur' – after E.T.A. Hoffman's 'Kater Murr' – as he was called affectionately) in February 1925. This was also the period of the great *poemy* (long poems) *Poem of the Mountain (Poema gory)* and *Poem of the End (Poema kontsa)*. These exalted and psychologically elaborate constructions seem to reflect some intense and passionate love affair – but the details of this are hazy, and there is some reason to suppose that the poems' basis in experience was slight, that more than anything else Tsvetayeva was "composing" life as well as poetry. This is not to say that there is anything false or artificial in the poems – rather that, as at other times in her life, Tsvetayeva used the raw material of her own existence in order to transcend it, to go beyond it. The relentless rhythms and jagged, leaping lines exude a recklessness of spirit, a Nietzschean disdain for the here and now:

Razom proigryvat' –
Chishche net!
Zagorod, prigorod:
Dnyam konets.

Negam (chitay – kamnyam),
Dnyam i domam i nam.

Dachi pustuyuschie! Kak mat'
Staruyu – tak zhe chtu ikh.
Eto ved' deystvie – pustovat':
Poloye ne pustuyet.

All at once to lose all –
No purer way.
Suburb, last port of call:
End of our days.

End to our joys (read millstones),
To days and houses and us.

Empty dachas! I have revered
You as might an aged mother.
It's hard work, after all, being empty there,
Being empty's not like being hollow.
(*Poem of the End*)

Poem of the End, like its mighty companion and predecessor, *Poem of the Mountain*, in some ways represents the apotheosis of Tsvetayeva's mature style. In it, stylistic, formal, and thematic elements unite in a stormy, almost savagely personal, yet nonethless universal song of exclusion, exile, and death: the separateness of the lovers acquires cosmic proportions, revealing a metaphysical chasm between soul and body, spirit and world. The poem's "Jewish" theme is also expanded to universal dimensions: Tsvetayeva, a lifelong enemy of anti-Semitism, who herself married a Jew, made her own sense of displacement from the status quo, the centre of things, her sense of the cosmic (and increasingly real) "suburb" or "ghetto" in which she found herself, into a declaration of the solidarity of poets with all outcasts, in all places and times:

Zá gorodom! Ponimayesh'? Za!
Vne! Pereshed val!
Zhizn', eto mesto, gde zhit' nel'zya:
Yev – reyskiy kvartal…

Tak ne dostoynee l' vó sto krat
Stat' vechnym zhidom?
Ibo dlya kazhdogo, kto ne gad,
Yev – reyskiy pogrom –

Zhizn'. Tol'ko vykrestami zhiva!
Iudami ver!
Na prokazhennyye ostrova!
V ad! – vsyudu! – no ne v

Zhizn' – tol'ko vykrestov terpit, lish'
Ovets – palachu!
Pravo-na-zhitel'stevennyy svoy list
No-gami topchu!

Vtaptyvayu! Za Davidov shchit –
Mest'! – V mesivo tel!
Ne upoitel'no li,chto zhid
Zhit' – né zakhotel?!

Getto izbránnichestv! Val i rov.
Po-shchady ne zhdi!
V syom khristianneyshem iz mirov
Poety – zhidy!

Out of town! Understand? Out! You must move
Beyond! You've crossed on your own!
Life is the place where no one may live:
It's the Jewish zone.

So isn't it a hundred times more noble
To become an eternal Jew?
Since for everyone who's not wholly a reptile
Life is equal to

A pogrom of Jews! Life's for converts,
The Judases of faith.
Go to hell, the penal islands, anywhere,
But not to life,

That spares only the traitor, the lamb
For the executioner's knife
On this document I stamp,
On my ticket to life.

I crush it. In vengeance for David's shield,
Into the mangled bodies' mess.
It's intoxicating that a Jew refused life,
That he didn't say yes?

Expect no mercy. The ghetto enfolds
The chosen few.
In this most Christian of worlds
The poet's a Jew.
('Poem of the End')

It says something important about this critical episode in Tsvetayeva's life as an artist that she began around the same time to work on prose – partly because it was easier to "sell" than poetry, but partly also, one suspects, because it provided some relief from the crushing demands of being a poet. It was in Czechoslovakia that she wrote the diary account of the revolution and civil war, *Earthly Traits (Zemnyye primety)*.

Although the intellectual and artistic atmosphere of Prague was very lively, it did not satisfy Tsvetayeva. She longed to be in Paris, where she believed there would be more opportunities for her to publish her poetry and articles and also to give readings in public. As more than one commentator has pointed out, Tsvetayeva could easily have found some kind of permanent employment – she had an excellent knowledge of both French and German. Yet she seems to have shared with Mandelstam an inability to "sell herself", to have a "job". Her attempts in that direction during her Moscow years are the best testimony to this. She evidently considered that she was a poet and only a poet, and that her only means of making a living was through literary work. This she was denied, not only in Soviet Russia, but also in the emigration – her unconventional, uncompromising personality made her many enemies on both sides of the literary-political barricades. She lived largely on the charity of friends; her letters are full of requests for money or thanks for it. Among those who helped Tsvetayeva financially during her Paris years were Anna Teskovà, Prince D.S. Svyatopolk-Mirsky, and Princess S.N. Halpern-Andronikova – the 'Solominka' of Mandelstam's poem of that title.

Just as Tsvetayeva never really lived for long in Prague itself, her Paris years were largely spent in the suburbs of that city. From 1925 onwards, she and Efron lived in a number of grey, depressing apartments in the vicinity of Meudon and Bellevue. Efron's time was increasingly taken up with political work: with the passage of time, his ardent Russian nationalism had carried him from association with right-wing circles to a growing interest in those circles in the emigration which advocated a return to the Soviet Union, and a greater Soviet motherland, which would incorporate both Europe and Asia. The 'Eurasians', to whose organisation Efron belonged, had close links with Moscow and the Soviet secret police. Tsvetayeva's children, too, began to grow away from her. Ariadna started to work for the Soviet-owned Paris newspaper *Nash Soyuz* (Our Union).

In Paris, Tsvetayeva published the last of her books she was to see in print during her lifetime. This was the collection *Posle Rossii* (After Russia), which appeared in 1928 and which represents a continuation and extension of the style and contents of *Remeslo*. The influence of Rainer Maria Rilke, whom Tsvetayeva had never met, but with whom she and Pasternak corresponded in the years immediately preceding the Austrian poet's death in 1927, is closely observable. Tsvetayeva attempts to construct a Rilkean mytho-poetic universe, as elaborated by Rilke in his *Neue Gedichte* and *Sonette an Orpheus*, a timeless and placeless sphere of intimately recollected detail, transformed by the poet's insight, redeemed by his sacrifice, and incorporated into the universal spirit of creation. In Tsvetayeva's poems, figures drawn from Hellenic and Biblical tradition mingle with characters from Middle High German literature and from Shakespeare. The tragic dimension is foremost, as in the sombre 'Deuce' *('Dvoye')*, dedicated to Pasternak:

Ne suzhdeno, chtoby sil'nyy s sil'nym
Soyedinilis' by v mire syom.
Tak razminulis' Zigfrid s Brungil'doy
Brachnoye delo reshiv mechom.

For strong with strong to be united
Is not willed by fate in this world.
Thus Siegfried and Brunhild decided
Their marital case with the sword.

In Paris, Tsvetayeva wrote some important long poems *(Poem of the Staircase, Poem of the Air, An Attempt at a Room)* and also some notable poem cycles, including, at the very end of her time in the West, the *Poems to Chekhia*, written in anger and despair at the partition of Czechoslovakia and its invasion by the Germans. More and more, however, she was involved in the writing of prose. As already mentioned, she believed that somehow she could "sell" her prose pieces and stories to an extent that was impossible with her poetry. Although she did succeed in selling some of the prose she wrote to émigré magazines and journals, her increasingly exclusive preoccupation with the medium meant that poetry came to have less and less place in her life.

Tsvetayeva's life in Paris during the 1930s had something of a nightmarish quality. On the political front, the world was becoming darker and darker. Tsvetayeva was almost completely isolated in the emigration – her husband's involvement with pro-Soviet circles meant that she was ostracised by many families. Moreover, she found herself increasingly at the mercy of the political and religious-ideological cliques that dominated the literary life of the Paris emigration between the wars; a "greeting" to Mayakovsky she had published in a literary journal when the Soviet poet visited Paris in 1928 was taken to imply her sympathy for the Soviet régime, and made it more and more difficult for her to find journals where she could have her work printed; in addition, the number of Russian-language émigré journals began to diminish under the effects of the harsh economic climate, until by the end of the 1930s there were hardly any left. In the spring of 1937, Ariadna returned to the Soviet Union. Finally, in the autumn of the same year, the Soviet defector Ignaz Reiss, a former White Army officer and opponent of the *vozvrashchentsy*, those who wished to organise a return to the Soviet Union, was found murdered on a country road near Lausanne in Switzerland. Efron disappeared from Paris, accused by the Swiss authorities of having helped commit the murder (the case was eventually dropped for lack of evidence). It was, however, later discovered that he was in Moscow, thus confirming the worst suspicions of the émigré community. The events of the autumn of 1938 and the spring of 1939 – the Munich agreement and the subsequent German invasion of Czechoslovakia – were more than Tsvetayeva could bear. The two countries which, after Russia, she loved most dearly and which might have provided her with refuge were now transformed into tyrant and bleeding victim – her last poem cycle *Poems to Chekhia* is a cry of rage and despair at a world gone mad. She had no choice: everything pushed her in one direction – towards Russia. During the civil war, when separated from Efron, Tsvetayeva had written to him in a letter which she was never able to send and an extract from which she had published in her prose memoir *Oktyabr v vagone* (October in a Railway Carriage): 'If God will perform that miracle – leave you among the living – I will follow you like a dog.' Tsvetayeva's copy of the issue of the journal *Volya Rossii*, in which the memoir was published, bears a handwritten note dated 21 April 1938: 'Now I will go: like a dog.' She said that when she climbed onto the deck of the steamship that was to take her to Russia she 'knew then that all was lost'.

Tsvetayeva and her son arrived in Moscow on 18 June 1939. Tsvetayeva was now 45. They settled in Bolshevo, near Moscow, where Efron was living in a communal villa belonging to the Soviet

Ministry of Foreign Affairs. Ariadna was seldom at home: she had a job on the Soviet French-language magazine *Revue de Moscou*, for which she wrote articles and did illustrations. At the end of August Ariadna and Efron were arrested by the Soviet secret police. They never saw Marina again. And thus her "reason" for returning to Russia was taken away.

The Bolshevo villa was sealed up, and Tsvetayeva found herself with her son on the street. She began to wander all over Moscow in search of lodgings. The only place she could find was a room in a house which was situated next door to the House of Writers (the Writers' Union club). Tsvetayeva had to pay full price for the room she rented, and had to find extra money to pay for heating. She received none of the discounts available to members of the Union. The only benefit she and Mur derived from living next door to the building was that they could eat in its modestly-priced refectory.

Tsvetayeva found that she could earn only pennies by her literary work. She was temperamentally unsuited to hackwork and worked very slowly on the translations (of ballads about Robin Hood, poems by Mickiewicz, Belorussian poets) which Pasternak helped to find for her. Often she went hungry. There is a story that when she was invited out to supper, she would appear with a string bag which she would then proceed to fill with food to take home with her. But most terrible of all was the loneliness she experienced. When she returned to Russia, it was in the expectation of making contact with some kindred souls, people who would understand the poetry she had written and who would respond to it. The two poets with whom she expected to find this kind of rapport were Nikolay Aseyev and Boris Pasternak. She was sorely disappointed. By this time, Aseyev had become an important literary functionary and leading light in the Writers' Union. The story is that he spoke to Tsvetayeva for some 15 minutes, and then tried to get away from his visitor as soon as possible, embarrassed and frightened to be seen talking to her. As for Pasternak: whether it was because, as some have said, he was afraid of his wife's jealousy, or because he had become disenchanted with Tsvetayeva's poetry, he did little to help bring her within the sphere of his considerable influence. The extent of his help was to find her occasional translation work. This was not enough for Tsvetayeva, whose soul cried out for a shoulder to lean on, for moral support.

A few people did listen to her, and invited her to their homes. Among these were the literary memoirists Ye. Ye. and Ye. B. Tager, who left a moving account of Tsvetayeva's presence in their household. She would write at their writing desk and read her poems to them in the evenings. She also managed to gain admittance to the local *gruppkom* of writers – the lowliest of the writers' organisations. But her poetry received absolutely no official recognition whatsoever, and a collection of poems she submitted to the State Publishing House in 1941 received an insulting reader's report by Kornely Zelinsky (later notorious for his role in the Pasternak affair).

Tsvetayeva found it difficult to relate to her son, Mur. Mur had been brought up in the West and had little liking for the new circumstances among which he was constrained to live. By nature self-willed and demanding, he made Tsvetayeva's life even more full of strain than it might otherwise have been. Tsvetayeva loved her son very much, and did everything she could for his sake. When war broke out, Tsvetayeva was terrified for Mur's safety, and insisted that they should be evacuated together into the country. Pasternak tried to dissuade Tsvetayeva from this step – he had some inkling of how difficult her life in evacuation would be. Nonetheless, she and Mur, then aged 16½, boarded a Volga steamship with other writers' families, bound for Kazan' and Chistopol'. Lidia Chukovskaya, the memoirist and wife of the poet Korney Chukovsky, recalls how in the course of the voyage Tsvetayeva kept returning to the subject of suicide. 'What can you be thinking of?' Chukovskaya remembers replying – 'I have two children to look after.' According to Chukovskaya, Tsvetayeva's retort to this was: 'But I know that my son will be better off without me....'

The boat reached Kazan', and then Chistopol', where most of the writers' families got out. Tsvetayeva was not permitted to disembark there, however, and she and Mur went further, to the even more remote Yelabuga. Here she tried to find work, without success. She wrote to the Tartar Union of Writers with a plea for translation work. No reply came. On 31 August 1941, Marina Tsvetayeva hanged herself in Yelabuga. No one has borne witness to her funeral, and the exact location of her grave in Yelabuga Cemetery is unknown.

Notes

1. Compare, for example, the gusting rhythmical (and untranslatable) music of Bely's *Vesel'e na Rusi* (Russian Revels) of 1906 with so many of Tsvetayeva's poems of nearly 20 years later, in particular some sections of *Poem of the End*. The Bely poem ends with a characteristic alternation of long and short rhythmic units:

Raskidalas' v vetre, plyashet –
Polevaya zherd': –

Vetkoy khlopayushchey mashet
Pryamo v tverd'.

Biryuzovoyu volnoyu
Nezhit tverd'.

Nad stranoy moyey rodnoyu
Vstala Smert'.

Sprawling in the wind – and dancing –
Pole in the field: –

Waving like a squelching treebranch
Straight at the earth.

Like a wave of turquoise
pampering the earth.

Above the land where I was born
Has arisen Death.

The effect finds a clear echo in lines such as these, from *Poem of the End*:

Pro – gal glubok:
Poslednego krov'yu greyu
Pro – slushay bok!
Ved' eto kuda vernee

Sti – khov... Progret
Ved'? Zavtra k komu naymyosh'sya?
Ska – zhi, chto bred!

Kon – tsa...
– Konets.

It's deep in this glade:
I warm it with the last blood of my body.
Feel my side.
After all, at least it's more steady

Than verses... Warm through
Now? Who'll you be kissing tomorrow night?
Tell me it's not true,
That the bridge is, will always be without

Its end...
– End.

2. A Moscow publishing house which also functioned as a debating society and centre for literary and anthropological studies.

3. *Svoimi putyami* (biograficheskiy ocherk), in *M. Tsvetayeva, Stikhotvoreniya i proza I*, Russica 1980, pp. [11] – [12].

4. These have been published in numerous Russian literary journals both in the USSR and in the West, and collected in *Ariadna Sergeyevna Efron: Stranitsy vospominaniy*, Paris, Izd. Lev, 1979.

Note on translating Tsvetayeva

Tsvetayeva is not an easy poet to translate into any language. The Russianness of her poetic style is something that defies transposition into another linguistic and cultural idiom. Her poems are rooted in the rhythms and patterns of Russian speech, yet they go beyond that speech toward a cosmic language of their own. Joseph Brodsky has characterised Tsvetayeva's poetry in the following words: 'If you could conjure up a combination of Hart Crane and Hopkins, that would be something like Tsvetayeva.' Something like her, that is, minus the Russian language.

Like Rainer Maria Rilke, a poet with whom she felt a lifelong bond and sympathy, although they never met, Tsvetayeva strove constantly beyond the limits of the "real" world. Whereas Rilke experienced this transcendence in terms of the visual and the spatial, for Tsvetayeva it was an *aural*, a musical experience – she heard, quite literally, the music of the spheres. This is not to say that there is anything abstract or wanly ethereal about her poems – they sing out of the flesh and blood of the poet, out of her lived life. But their élan, their essential movement is all in a rush towards another world.

The rhymes and rhythms of Tsvetayeva's poems serve a dual function: they are her main compositional device, and they also play an emblematic, even a symbolic role:

> In this world there are rhymes.
> Disjoin them – and it trembles.

I believe it is necessary for any translator of Tsvetayeva's poetry to make at least some attempt to reproduce the formal and structural attributes of her poems, even though it is an attempt that is forever doomed to failure. Not to try is, it seems to me, to ignore the very heart, the central meaning of Tsvetayeva's work. Without their forms, their harmonies and discords, Tsvetayeva's poems are simply – not there. The versions that follow make no pretence at being finished poems. They are offered in the hope that they may give to the reader of English some idea of what a Tsvetayeva poem looks and sounds like. Above all, my translations are offered in what I conceive to be the Tsvetayevan spirit.

DAVID McDUFF

POEMS OF YOUTH

1913-18

B

This gypsy passion

This gypsy passion for parting!
We just meet, but already take flight!
My brow's in my hands, I'm starting
To think, looking out through the night

That those who ransack our letters
Have only perceived by halves
How faithless we are, and that is –
How faithful we are to ourselves.

[October 1915]

With great tenderness

With great tenderness – because it's true
I'll soon forsake you all –
I'm trying to determine who
Shall have my wolfskin stole,

Who shall have my pampering plaid,
My slender borzoi cane,
And my silver bracelet sprayed
With drops of turquoise rain...

And all the notes, the flowers that I'm
Unable to hold tight...
Who will inherit my last rhyme,
Who'll inherit you – my last night.

[22 September 1915]

You that make your way

You that make your way past me aspire
Toward charms not my own, not genuine –
Oh, if only you knew how much fire,
How much life had been wasted on nothing,

And what ardent heroics and dash
Went on casual wraiths and chatter –
How my heart was converted to ash
By this senselessly dusted-on powder.

O fast trains flying into the dark,
Taking sleep away at the station…
Yet I know: even then off the mark,
You would not have the slightest notion

Why my words have such tautness and strain
In my cigarette smoke's ceaseless swirling –
How much dark and menacing pain
Fills my head with its hair's light curling.

[17 May 1913]

For my poems

For my poems, written down so soon in life, so early
I did not know I was a poet yet,
Forced loose from me like droplets from a fountain,
A rocket's sparking jet,

Poems storming from me, invading, like some tiny demons
The sanctuary where sleep and incense twine,
Their themes made up of youth and death, my poems,
My always unread lines!

Thrown here and there amid the dust of various bookshops,
Untouched then, now, by any reader's thumb,
For my poems, stored deep like wines of precious vintage,
I know a time will come.

[Koktebel', May 1913]

Some forebear of mine

Some forebear of mine was a violinist,
A horseman and thief, moreover.
Isn't that where I got my wanderlust,
Why my hair smells of wind and weather?

Swarthy, guiding my hand, is it not really him
Stealing apricots from the fruit-cart?
Curly-haired, hook-nosed, is it not his whim
That my fate is all passion and hazard?

Admiring the tiller at his plough,
In his lips he twirled a sweet-brier.
He made a perfidious friend, but how
Dashing and tender a lover.

Of moon, pipe and beads he was long a fan,
And of all female neighbours…
It seems to me he was a cowardly man,
My yellow-eyed, distant forebear.

That after he'd sold the devil his life
He'd not walk through the graveyard at midnight.
It occurs to me, too, that he carried a knife
Hidden inside his bootflap.

That many a time from round some fence
He'd leap, a supple feline.
And somehow it was I came to sense
He didn't play his violin.

Like last year's snow in summer's days
All had lost its meaning for him.
That's the kind of fiddler my forebear was.
That's the kind of poet I am.

[22 June 1915]

Much like me

Much like me, you make your way forward,
Walking with downturned eyes.
Well, I too kept mine lowered.
Passer-by, stop here, please.

Read, when you've picked your nosegay
Of henbane and poppy flowers,
That I was once called Marina,
And discover how old I was.

Don't think that there's any grave here,
Or that I'll come and throw you out...
I myself was too much given
To laughing when one ought not.

The blood hurtled to my complexion,
My curls wound in flourishes...
I *was*, passer-by, I existed!
Passer-by, stop here, please.

And take, pluck a stem of wildness,
The fruit that comes with its fall –
It's true that graveyard strawberries
Are the biggest and sweetest of all.

All I care is that you don't stand there,
Dolefully hanging your head.
Easily about me remember,
Easily about me forget.

How rays of pure light suffuse you!
A golden dust wraps you round...
And don't let it confuse you,
My voice from under the ground.

[Koktebel', 3 May 1913]

Every poem is a child of love

Every poem is a child of love,
A waif born illegitimately.
A first-born, set at the mercy of
The wind, beside the railway.

For the heart, both altar and hell.
For the heart, both heaven and grief.
The father? Maybe a tsar, who can tell,
A tsar, or maybe a thief.

[14 August 1918]

I'm happy to live like a paragon

I'm happy to live like a paragon, plainly
As the sun, the pendulum, the calendar,
To be a worldly anchorite, shapely
And wise – as all God's creatures are.

To know that the Spirit's my partner, my mentor.
To come in unannounced, like a look, like a light.
To live as I write: like a paragon, tersely,
A God has ordained and my friends won't permit.

[22 November 1918]

Bring me what others don't require

Bring me what others don't require.
All must burn upon my fire!
I entice life, I entice death,
Simple gifts to my fire's breath.

The flames love fragile substances:
Last year's illness, garlands, sentences...
Food like that makes the flames soar!
Purer than ash you'll rise once more!

A Phoenix, only in fire I sing!
To my life bring succour, buttressing!
I burn up tall, and I burn up quite,
And may the night for you be light.

Bonfire of ice, fountain of flame!
Aloft I bear my lofty frame,
Aloft I bear my lofty name:
Interlocutor and Inheritor!

[2 September 1918]

My horse

My horse is all-consuming fire –
He doesn't neigh, his hooves don't rear.
Where my horse breathes, springs will not flow,
Where my horse prances, grass won't grow.

Oh fire my horse – you tireless eater!
Oh fire my horse – you tireless rider!
My hair's mixed with his mane, and flies,
A stripe of flame, into the skies.

[14 August 1918]

BON-VOYAGES

1921-22

I bless the daily labour

I bless the daily labour of my hands,
I bless the sleep that nightly is my own.
The mercy of the Lord, the Lord's commands,
The law of blessings and the law of stone.

My dusty purple, with its ragged seams…,
My dusty staff, where all light's rays are shed.
And also, Lord, I bless the peace
In others' houses – others' ovens' bread.

[21 May 1918]

From Bon Voyages

(to Osip Mandelstam)

Seeing off the beloved ones, I
Give them songs, so that we get even
Through these tokens which may supply
Them again with what I was given.

By the overgrown lane at noon
I'd lead them to the juncture, where...
You, the wind, sing your tireless tune,
You, the road, treat their steps with care.

Dove-blue cloud, don't shed your tears:
Spare their Sunday best for good weathers!
Coiling dragon, clamp tight your teeth,
Drop, you bully-boys, your sly razors.

You, a beauty in passage, be
A gay bride for them, do a favour:
Strain your lips for a while for me:
You'll be paid by the Precious Saviour!

Go, bonfires, light up dark trees,
Drive each animal to its lair.
Virgin Mary in heaven, please,
For my passers-by – say a prayer.

[February 1916]

translated by F.F. MORTON

Make merry, my soul

Make merry, my soul, drink and eat!
When my last hour goes
Stretch me so that my two feet
Cover four high roads.

Where, the empty fields across,
Wolves and ravens roam,
Over me make the shape of a cross,
Signpost looming alone.

In the night I have never shunned
Places accursed and blamed.
High above me you shall stand,
Cross without a name.

Many of you were wined and fed
By me, companions, friends.
Cover me over with your head,
Snowstorm of the fens.

Do not light a candle for me
In the church's depth.
I don't want eternal memory
On my native earth.

[4 April 1916]

God stooped

God stooped from his labour earnestly
And grew calm.
Then he smiled, created many
Holy angels in a swarm,

Their bodies made of radiant, luminous
Shimmerings.
Some have wings that are enormous,
But there are some that have no wings.

Due to this I am tear-swollen,
Due to this:
More than with God, I've fallen
In love with those angels of his.

[15 August 1916]

From Insomnia

After a sleepless night the body weakens.
It grows dear, not one's own, it's nobody's.
Sluggish, the veins still retain an ache of arrows,
One smiles to all with a seraph's ease.

After a sleepless night the hands weaken.
Deeply indifferent are both friend and enemy.
Each casual sound contains an entire rainbow.
And the frost smells of Florence suddenly.

Lips glow softly, the shadow's more golden
Under sunken eyes. Night has set ablaze
This most radiant countenance – and dark night renders
But one part of us dark – the eyes.

[19 July 1916]

No one has taken away anything

No one has taken away anything.
I savour our separateness.
I kiss you across the hundreds
Of disuniting versts.

I know our gifts are not even.
My voice is calm, for the first time.
What good to you, young Derzhavin,
Are my undisciplined rhymes?

For your fearsome flight I christen you:
Young eagle, you must fly on.
You suffered the sun, unblinking,
Does my young gaze weigh you down?

No one watched more stalwart and tender
Than I as you disappeared.
I kiss you across the hundreds
Of disuniting years.

[12 February 1916]

From the cycle Poems to Akhmatova

2

My hands grasping my head, I stand.
What of human scheming!
I sing, my head grasped in my hands,
In the dawn's late gleaming.

Ah, a violent breaker threw
Me to sixes and sevens.
I sing you, because we've one of you,
As we've one moon in the heavens.

Because a raven you flew into a heart
Piercing the grey clouds' blindness.
You're hook-nosed, and your anger's a dart
Of death, as is your kindness.

Because you covered with your night
My Kremlin's pure gold ringing,
Winding a strap around my throat
You choked me with your singing.

Ah, I am fortunate! Never yet
Has any dawn shone purer.
I'm fortunate! Giving all I've got
To you, I leave – a beggar.

And you whose voice – dark vertigo –
Drew all my breathing tighter,
I called you Muse of Tsarskoye Selo,
And first gave you that title.

[22 June 1916]

3

They sleep, one last giant stroke conferred
On air, those lashes.
Beloved body! O bird
Most weightless, ashes.

What did she do in the mist of days?
Waited, sang a melody.
In her were so many sighs,
Scant flesh and body.

She sleeps. A choir draws her inside
The gardens of Eden.
As if songs left her unsatisfied:
Drowsing demon!

Hours, years, centuries.
Not a trace of us, our four walls.
The monument, growing roots,
No longer recalls.

The broom has lain unused since long ago,
And the nettles' crosses
Over the Muse of Tsarskoye Selo
Droop full of praises.

[23 June 1916]

SWANS' ENCAMPMENT

POEMS

1917-1921

From the church so austere and shapely

From the church so austere and shapely,
You came out to the shriek of the square.
Freedom! The Beautiful Lady
Whom marquis and Russian prince share.

The fearsome choir-practice is growling.
Ahead the service waits.
Freedom! – a harlot sprawling
In a maddened soldier's embrace.

[26 May 1917]

From André Chénier

André Chénier went to the block to die.
But I'm alive – and that's a grievous sin.
There are times that are made of iron.
He's not a bard who sings when bullets fly.

He's not a father who, from his son's head,
Trembling, tears the warrior's helmeting.
There are times where the sun's a deadly sin.
He's not a man who in our day's not dead.

[Theodosia, April 1918]

Wretched are the strong and the wealthy

Wretched are the strong and the wealthy.
On their lordships a heavy weight lies.
But whenever I meet a soldier
I don't lower my bright, clear eyes.

The city groans in its turbulence.
The moon's lost in a wine-froth stour.
But no one lays a finger on me:
I am arrogant and poor.

[Theodosia, end of October 1917]

We must declare ourselves boldly, lyre

We must declare ourselves boldly, lyre.
For the great of the world we have felt desire:
For masts, for banners, for churches, for tsars:
For sages, for heroes, for eagles and bards.
Thus, swearing you're loyal to the Tsars and their lands,
You don't abandon their Tent to the winds.

If you know the Tsar, you don't favour his page.
Our loyalty's held us, an anchorage,
Loyalty to his greatness, by guilt weighed down,
Loyalty to the great guilt of his crown.
As we swear allegiance to the Khan
We do not swear the same to his Horde.

A windy age, lyre, lashes our heads,
The wind rips our uniforms into shreds,
Fluttering somewhere, last rag of the Tent.
But we remain faithful to our vow,
For winds are bad lords whom no heed should be lent.

[1 August 1918]

White is a threat to Blackness's field

White is a threat to Blackness's field.
The white temple threatens coffins, threatens thunder,
The pale righteous man threatens Sodom, drives it under
Not with a sword – with lilies in his shield.

Whiteness! Your circle's not made by hand of man.
Baptismal font. A prophet's hair that's greying.
The world, the worm, both recognise their Sovereign
By the small flower that flowers from his hand.

Only to the angel will the fortress fall.
Only the lamb brings the wolf to the slaughter.
Triumph lurks in cellars and in thieves' corners,
As the White ranks ascend to the Capital.

[25 May 1918]

Night. Nor'-easter.

Night. Nor'-easter. Roar of soldiers. Roar of waves.
They have looted the wine depot. Along the walls,
Along the gutters a precious stream flows,
And in it, bloody, dances the moon.

The crazed pillars of the poplars.
The crazed singing of birds in the night.
Yesterday's monument to the Tsar stands bare.
And above the monument stretches the night.

The docks drink. The barracks drink. The world is ours.
Ours is all the wine of the princes' cellars.
The entire city, stampeding like a bull,
Falls down at the murky puddle to drink.

The moon is lost in a cloud of wine-froth. Who goes there?
Be it comrade or pretty girl: drink.
And a merry rumour circulates in town:
Somewhere two people have drowned in the wine.

[Theodosia, the last days of October]

NOTE: *The birds were drunk* – M.Ts.

White Guards

White Guards: Gordian knot
Of Russian valour.
White Guards: white mushrooms
Of the Russian folksong.
White Guards: white stars,
Not to be crossed from the sky.
White Guards: black nails
In the ribs of the Antichrist.

[27 June 1918]

All this is simple, as blood and sweat are

All this is simple, as blood and sweat are:
A Tsar for a people, a people for a Tsar.

All this is clear as two's secret, shared:
Two together – the Spirit's third.

The Tsar's raised from heaven upon his throne.
This is as pure as sleep and snow.

The Tsar will climb to his throne again, yet –
All this is holy, as blood and sweat.

[24 April 1918]

Easter Monday – and he had less than 3 months to live – M.Ts.

As you fought for your fatherland

As you fought for your fatherland
You scratched *Marina* on your knife.
I was the first and also the last
In all the magnificence of your life.

I remember the night and your brilliant face
Enclosed in a military boxcar's hell.
I let my hair fly in the wind's wild chase.
In a chest I store your epaulettes well.

[Moscow, 18 January 1918]

If the soul was born with pinions

If the soul was born with pinions
What are hovels to it, what are mansions?
What's Genghis Khan to it and what his Horde?
I have two enemies in all the world,
Two twins, inseparably fused:
The hunger of the hungry and the fullness of the full.

[18 August 1918]

Above the churchtower there are clouds of blue

Above the churchtower there are clouds of blue,
The caw of crows…
And there, of ashen, sandy hue,
The revolutionary troops pass through.
My lordly pain, my kingly anguish, you.

They're without faces, without names.
And without songs!
You've lost your way, Kremlin chimes,
Inside this windy wood of banners, deep.
Pray, Moscow. Lie down to eternal sleep.

[Moscow, 2 March 1917]

THE CRAFT

1923

From Girlhood

1

My girlhood! My estranged, my someone else's
Girlhood. My shoe without a mate.
Narrowing your eyes, red swollen,
As from a calendar you'd tear a date.

All you forced into your plunder's sack
Is left by my reflective Muse unwanted.
My girlhood, I won't try to call you back.
You've been a burden and a hindrance.

At nights *you* scoured me with your carding comb,
At nights *you* sharpened up your arrows.
Choked on *your* gifts as on a chip of stone,
I paid not for my sins, but someone else's.

I hand your sceptre back before it's time.
What, to the soul, are food and being full?
My girlhood! Mischief-maker, dark and gloom.
My girlhood! You were my red rag to the bull!

[14 November 1921]

2

Not for long a swallow, you'll soon be a witch.
My girlhood, let's say goodbye before the day on which
You leave, let's stand as the wind blows wild,
Console your sister, dusky child.

Blaze with all the crimson of your skirt,
My girlhood! My dusky bird!
Of my soul, the radiant dawn!
My girlhood, console me, then dance on!

Slash the heavens with your azure wrap,
My crazed one. Men filled their cup
With craziness because of you. Dance and scald!
Farewell, my amber – and my gold!

I touch your hands with a special end in view,
As to a lover, bid farewell to you.
Torn from breast of depths that lie deep below,
My girlhood, be gone. And to others, go.

[20 November 1921]

From The Disciple

2

There is a certain hour like a shed burden,
When in ourselves we tame our pride.
Hour of discipledom – in every lifetime
Triumphant, and not to be denied.

A lofty hour when, having laid our weapons
At feet shown to us by a pointing Hand,
We trade for camel hair our martial porphyry
Upon the sea's expanse of sand.

O this hour, like the Voice that raises
Us to greater deeds from the self-will of days!
O hour, when our dense volume presses on us
We bow to earth like the ripe ears of maize.

The ears have grown, the festive hour is over,
The grain is longing for the grinding mill
The Law! The Law! The yoke which in the earth's womb
I lust after still.

Hour of discipledom. But visible's
Another light – yet one more dawn has glowed.
Be blessed, and follow in its steps,
You, sovereign hour of solitude.

[15 April 1921]

AFTER RUSSIA

POEMS

1922-1925

In Praise of the Rich

Herewith, having warned you beforehand
That between us is many miles' space,
That I am one of the riff-raff,
And in life have an honest place:

Under the wheels of all excesses,
Host to hunchback and cripple, queer fish...
Herewith I shout from the rooftops,
Declare it – I *love* the rich.

For their root that is rotten, decrepit,
From the cradle growing its wound,
Their hands moving in unconscious habit
From their pockets, and to them returned.

For the softest requests that their mouths make,
Each obeyed like an ordering cry,
And because they won't get into heaven,
And won't look you straight in the eye.

For their secrets – by special delivery,
Their passions – by courier post,
For their nights, which are foisted upon them,
(Even kissing and drinking are forced!)

And because in their cotton-wool yawning,
Their gilding, their counting itch
They can't buy me, impudent upstart,
I affirm that I *love* the rich.

Never mind that shine, of the shaven,
That wined, dined look (I wink and it's mine),
It's that sudden look of the craven,
Those eyes with their doggy shine,

Doubting…
                        are the scales set at zero?
Are the weights not perhaps loaded short?
Because of all the world's outcasts
These are the sorriest sort.

An unpleasant fable informs us
How some camels pass through needle eyes.
…For their look of 'To *death* I'm astonished',
As they plead their infirmities

Like bankruptcy. 'I'd have lent…Been glad to'
…For their quiet words, mouthed with a twitch:
'I counted in carats, was a brother…'
I swear it: I *love* the rich.

[30 September 1922]

Grey Hairs

These are ashes of treasures:
Of hurt and loss.
These are ashes in face of which
Granite is dross.

Dove, naked and brilliant,
It has no mate.
Solomon's ashes
Over vanity that's great.

Time's menacing chalkmark,
Not to be overthrown.
Means God knocks at the door
– Once the house has burned down!

Not choked yet by refuse,
Days' and dreams' conqueror.
Like a thunderbolt – Spirit
Of early grey hair.

It's not you who've betrayed me
On the home front, years.
This grey is the triumph
Of immortal powers.

[17 September 1922]

From The Poet

2

The world has its unwanted extras
Who fall outside the eyeball's sweep
(Not featured in your works of reference,
For them, home is the rubbish heap).

The world has hollow creatures, jostled
And speechless, its cartload of shit.
Sharp nails to rip your silken hemline,
Mud for wheels to throw on it.

The world has fictions beyond vision.
(Their sign: the sores of leprosy!)
The world has Jobs who would have envied
Job each hour of his agony.

We're poets – rhyme with sewer rats –
But we rise from the murky flood,
Contend with every god for every goddess,
With every virgin for each god.

3

What is left for me, sightless and fatherless,
In this world where all have sight, a paternal home,
Where the passions must brave anathemas
Like trenches! Where weeping is
Called a head cold!

What is left for me, who by my nature, my knowledge,
Live to sing – like cables! tan! Siberian wastes!
Over my infatuations as over a bridge!
With their weightlessness
In a world of weights.

What am I to do, singer and first-born,
In a world where grey is the blackest that's found!
Where inspiration is kept as in thermos flasks!
With this boundlessness
In a world of bounds?

[22 April 1923]

The Hour of the Soul

1

At the deep hour of the soul and night,
Not figured yet on any clock,
Into a young boy's eyes I led my sight,
Not figured yet as a double lock

On the flow of nights for anyone,
Ponds filled to oblivion, to the rims,
And resting tranquilly.
                                        From now on
Your life gets underway, begins.

The greying Roman she-wolf's eye,
Espying in her nursling – Rome.
Dream-conjuring maternity
Of the rock... There is no name, no home

For my perplexities... I've shed
My every veil, have grown from loss.
Thus kneeling, bowing down her head
Over the wicker basket was

Egypt's daughter...

[14 July 1923]

2

At the deep hour of the soul,
Deep hour – nocturnal...
(Gigantic stride of the soul,
Soul in night's hold.)

At that hour, soul, rule all
The worlds you will
To govern – palaces of soul,
Soul, rule them all.

Make rusty your lips, with snow
Powder your lashes
(Atlantic sigh of soul,
Soul in night's hold...)

Soul, with darkness kohl
The eyes where like Vega
You arise... Of sweetest fruit
Make bitter gall.

Make bitter, dark as coal.
Grow great: and rule.

[8 August 1923]

3

For the soul there's an hour, as there is for the moon,
For the owl, the gloom, the dark.
For the soul there's an hour as there was for the tune,
In Saul's dreams, of David's harp...

Vanity, tremble at that hour,
Wash away your rouge and your shine.
For the soul there's an hour like the thundershower,
My child, and this hour is mine.

The hour of the breast's most precious depths,
The breaking of a dam.
All things are torn from familiar berths,
All secrets from each mouth's clam,

All veils from eyes. All footprints led
To their source. All the notes unstuck
From their staves. The soul's hours the hour of Dread,
My child, and that hour has struck.

'O Dread of mine.' That's what you'll croak.
Thus, tortured by the knife
The surgeon plies, children reproach
Their mother: 'Why are we alive?'

And she, with her hands' cool palms relieves
Their fever. 'It must be. Rest.'
'My child, the Soul's hour is like the knife's.
But the knife is blessed.'

[14 August 1923]

Deuce

1

In this world there are rhymes.
Disjoin them – and it trembles.
Homer, you were blind.
Night on your eyebrows' snowdrifts,

Night cloaked your rhapsodies.
Night, on your eyes, a curtain.
With sight, would you have dis-
joined Achilles and Helen?

Achilles, Helena.
Name music more harmonious.
For yes, in spite of chaos
It is on assonances

The world's built – disunited
It takes revenge (built on agreement!)
Through unfaithful wives' desertion,
Troy ablaze and incandescent.

You, rhapsodist, were blind.
You scattered rhymes like leavings.
There are rhymes that are designed
In the *other* world. If *this* collapses,

You'll divorce them. What need in
Rhyme? Helena, grow older.
...Noblest warrior of Achaea,
The sweetheart of all Sparta.

Only the myrtles' stir,
The lyre's sleep recite it:
'Achilles, Helena,
A couple disunited.'

2

For strong with strong to be united
Is not willed by fate in this world.
Thus Siegfried and Brunhild decided
Their marital case with the sword.

In the brotherly hate of their union
Like buffaloes! Stone against stone.
From the marriage bed he crept, unrecognised,
Unidentified, she slumbered on.

Apart – even on the bed of marriage –
Apart – even clenched like a fist –
Apart – in double digit language –
Apart-too-late – so our marriage is!

There is one older wickedness:
With the amazon crushed, lion-wild,
Achilles, the son of Thetis,
Missed his meeting with Ares' child,

Penthesilea.
O remember
Her look from below. The look of
The felled rider. Her look, not from Olympus –
From dungwash, yet still from above.

From that time he had no thought but this one,
To snatch his wife from murkiness.
Fate does not join equal with equal…
. . . .
We too passed without meeting like this.

3

In a world where all
Are bent-backed and asweat
I know one alone
Can equal my strength.

In a world where so much
Is left to desire
I know one alone
Can equal my power.

In a world where all
Is ivy, decaying,
I know one alone –
You – are equal in being

To me.

[3 July 1924]

The Demon in Me

The demon in me's not dead,
He's living, and well.
In the body as in a hold,
In the self as in a cell.

The world is but walls.
The exit's the axe.
('All the world's a stage,'
The actor prates.)

And that hobbling buffoon
Is no joker:
In the body as in glory,
In the body as in a toga.

May you live forever!
Cherish your life.
Only poets in bone
Are as in a lie.

No, my eloquent brothers,
We'll not have much fun.
In the body as with Father's
Dressing-gown on.

We deserve something better.
We wilt in the warm.
In the body as in a byre.
In the self as in a cauldron.

Marvels that perish
We don't collect.
In the body as in a marsh.
In the body as in a crypt.

In the body as in furthest
Exile. It blights.
In the body as in a secret.
In the body as in the vice

Of an iron mask.

[5 January 1925]

Beware

For two, even mornings'
Joy is too small.
As you choke inside
Turn your face to the wall

(For the Spirit's a pilgrim,
Walks alone its way),
Let your hearing drop
To the primal clay.

Adam, listen hard
Over the source,
Hear what rivers' veins
Are telling their shores.

You are the way and the end,
The path and the house.
By two no new lands
Can be opened out.

To the brows' lofty camp
You are bridge and breach.
(God is a despot,
Jealous of each).

Adam, listen hard
Over the source,
Hear what rivers' veins
Are telling their shores:

'Beware of your servant:
When the proud trump plays
Don't appear in our Father's house
Fettered, a slave.

Beware of your wife:
Casting off mortal things,
When the naked trump sounds
Don't appear wearing rings.'

Adam, listen hard
Over the source,
Hear what rivers' veins
Are telling their shores:

'Beware. Don't build towers
On closeness and kin.
(Far more firm than *her*
In our hearts is *Him*.)

Don't be tempted by eagles.
King David still cries
To this day for his son
Who fell into the skies.'

Adam, listen hard
Above the source,
Hear what rivers' veins
Are telling their shores:

'Beware of graves,
More ravenous than whores.
The dead rot, they are gone,
Beware sepulchres.

From yesterday's truths
Remain filth and stench.
Give up to the winds
Your earthly ash.'

Adam, listen hard
Over the source,
Hear what rivers' veins
Are telling their shores:

'Beware.'

[8 August 1922]

The Window

In the sweet, Atlantic
Breathing of spring
My curtain's like a butterfly,
Huge, fluttering

Like a Hindu widow
To a pyre's golden blaze,
Like a drowsy Naïad
To past-window seas.

[5 May 1923]

UNCOLLECTED POEMS

I will win you away from every earth, from every sky

I will win you away from every earth, from every sky,
For the woods are my place of birth, and the place to die,
For while standing on earth, I touch it with but one foot,
For I'll sing your worth as nobody could or would.

I will win you from every time and from every night,
From all banners that throb and shine, from all swords held tight,
I'll drive dogs outside, hurl the keys into dark and fog,
For in the mortal night I'm a more faithful dog.

I will win you from all my rivals, and from the one,
You will never enjoy a bridal, nor I – a man,
And in the final struggle I'll take you – don't make a sound! –
From Him by whom Jacob stood on the darkened ground.

But until I cross your fingers upon your breast,
You possess – what a curse! – yourself: you are self-possessed,
Both your wings, as they yearn for the ether, become unfurled,
For the world's your cradle, and your grave's the world.

[15 August 1916]

translated by F.F. MORTON

Nailed against the shameful stake

Nailed against the shameful stake
Of the inveterate Slavic conscience,
My forehead marked, at my heart a snake,
I testify that I am guiltless.

I testify that in me is the calm
Communicants know before communion,
That it's not my fault if with palm
Outstretched on squares I stand – for fortune!

Examine all my earthly goods and say
– Are my eyes stricken with blindness? –
Where is my gold? The silver that's for me?
In my palm is a fistful of ashes.

This is all that with flattery and prayer
I have coaxed from those whom fortune blesses.
And this is all that I'll take with me there,
Into the land of silent embraces.

[19 May 1920]

Bush

1

What does it need from me, this bush?
Not speech. Not my dog's destiny
Of a human, to curse which I push
My head (growing greyer each day)

In its leaves, to hide it away.
So thick, so matted, so taut.
What does this bush need from me?
One who has, from one who has not?

It needs something. Or it wouldn't have poured
Into my thoughts, ears, eyes, my all.
If it didn't, it wouldn't have flowered
Straight into my wide-open soul,

Which only of bush isn't bare:
Window on all my godforsaken places,
O full cup of bush, hear:
What do you find in these wildernesses?

What didn't they spy there, your looks
(If one leaf were the same on your branches!)
In all my stumbling blocks,
Riddled, punctuated masses?

What didn't you hear there (speech walks
In your boughs, is not born of torture)
In all my stumbling blocks,
Riddled, punctuated noises?

And now, when I have betrayed
To the dictionary my immortal power,
Is it really true that what I say
Is what I knew before

I opened my mouth, on the boundary
Of my lips – behind which are fragments...
And will know again in entirety
As soon as I've run out of eloquence.

2

And for me, from the bush (not so much
Noose for a bit, world of man),
And for me from the bush there's a hush:
Between silence and speaking, a span.

You may call that hush nothing, or all,
It is deep and it is unavoidable.
Puzzlements! Of our posthumous poems,
The miraculous puzzle.

Puzzle of ancient gardens.
Puzzle of new musical art.
Puzzle of one's very first words.
Puzzle of Faust's Second Part.

That which stands after all, and before:
Noise of crowds in their forumward run.
Puzzle of blood's roaring in the ear,
In which all combines into one

As if all the pitchers of the East
Had been poured on my forehead's hill.
From the bush such quietness,
One can't say it more fully: it's full.

[August 1934]

Table

1

My writing, faithful table!
Thank you – with me you travelled
All paths, however far,
Protecting me, like a scar.

My writing, packload mule,
Thank you – your legs stood cruel
Burdens of dreams and lore.
Thank you – you bore and bore.

Mirror of greatest severity!
Thank you for getting in the way
(Threshold to worldly ploys)
Of all of my life's joys,

And all its pains – point blank!
A counterweight, oak plank
Against all: the lion of hate,
The elephant of hurt.

My vitally dead board
Thank you for growing forward
With me, I watched you and
My tablework expand,

Extend to a latitude
Where, grasping at your wood
Agape, I felt you pour
On me as on a shore.

Having nailed me to you at daybreak,
Thank you for darting
After me! On every path
You caught me, like a shah

A fugitive.
'Back to your chair.'
Thank you – you steered me with care
Away from unlasting joys
Like a hypnotist magus his

Somnambulist.
Table, you made
My battle-scars a balustrade
Of fire: crimson of veins.
Column of deeds and pains.

Stylites' column, of lips the seal,
My throne, my open field.
For me you've been the same
As the Hebrews' pillar of flame.

Then blessed, blessed be.
Tested by shoulder and knee
And brow, table, saw-edge pressed,
Eating into my breast.

[July 1933]

2

The thirtieth anniversary
Of our union, more faithful than love.
I know your every wrinkle
As you know mine and of

Which you, are you not the author?
Having eaten quire after quire,
Teaching there's no tomorrow,
That today is all there is here.

Table, hurling money and letters
The mailman brings, into the fray.
Insisting that the deadline
For every line is today.

Threatening that counting of cutlery
Doesn't give the Creator his due,
That tomorrow they will stretch me,
Poor idiot woman, on you.

3

The thirtieth anniversary
Of our union. Get back, knaves!
I know your every wrinkle,
Your flaws, your toothmarks and grooves,

The slightest of your notches
(Made with *teeth* if I failed in my task).
Yes, a fellow creature was loved,
And this creature was a desk

Of pine. Not for me the hilliness
Of birch, from the Karelian shore.
Sometimes you wept tears of resin
But then, overnight, grew more

Mature – as a schoolboy's insolence
Gives way to a man's firm hand.
I sit down – your boards hold out scarcely, –
Take you on like a lifelong friend.

You standing straight, I bending
My back – write, write!
How many acres we covered,
How many miles put to flight,

Covered with writing more handsome
Than you'll find in all the land.
Not less than half of Russia
Has been covered by this hand.

A pine table, oak table, tuppenny
Lacquered one, ring in its nose,
A garden one, dining one, any
But on three legs, not one of those.

That one, like the altar where my namesake
Took my False Demetriuses three.
A billiard, bazaar table, any
Just so long as it doesn't betray

The secret heights. An *iron*
One, holding two elbows through
Their toil – cornucopia of tables!
Stump too broad to be hugged by two.

And the church porch? The circular well-rim?
The smooth pellicle of the grave?
If only my two elbows
Would always say: God will give,

God *is*. The poet's inventive,
The world's his table, his altar and throne.
But better than all, most enduring
Are you – table scarred by my pen.

[*Approx.* 15 July 1933 – 29-30 October 1935]

I've dissolved for you

I've dissolved for you, in that glass over there,
A handful of my burnt hair.
So there will be no singing, no eating,
So there will be no drinking, no sleeping.

So your youth will lose its freshness,
And your sugar will lose its sweetness.
So at night you'll be locked in strife
With your young wife.

As my golden tresses
Have turned to grey ashes,
So your young years will be quite
Turned to winter, white.

So your ear will go deaf, and blind your eye,
So like moss you will become dry,
So you will vanish like a sigh.

[3 November 1918]

House

From under frowning, knitted brows
As if it were my girlhood's day, the house
Greets me, as if it might even be
My youth itself: 'Hello, I!'

So near, familiar is the way
Its forehead hides itself away
Under the ivy that's growing on top,
As if embarrassed at being grown up.

Not without reason – 'Carry! Load!' –
In the never-drying mud
Of all the backwaters where I've had
To live, my brow's seemed a façade,
The Apollonian lift to the sky
Of the museum's façade, created by

My forehead. Far from all byways,
Behind my poems I'll end my days,
As if behind an elder's boughs.

My eyes hold no warmth: green, could pass
For green of antique window glass,
A hundred years spying grounds that have
Stood here a century and a half.

The panes, as somnolent as sleep,
Of windows with one law they keep:
Guests are what they must not expect,
Strangers what they must not reflect.

Not yielding to day's bitterness,
These eyes that have remained here: eyes,
Reflecting mirrors of themselves.

From under frowning, knitted brows,
O greenness of my girlhood's days!

Green of my dress and of my beads,
Green of my eyes, green of my tears…
In the encircling giants' span
House, survival, nobleman.
Concealed inside the lime grove's shape,
The maidenly daguerrotype

Of my soul.

[6 September 1931]

United as the left hand and the right

United as the left hand and the right
Your soul and mine are fixed together, tight.

We're warm and blissful, neighbouring
Like a left-sided and right-sided wing.

But then a storm comes – and a gaping cleft
Is made between the right wing and the left.

[10 July 1918]

Longing for the motherland

Longing for the motherland. A mystery
Whose laws I've long ago penetrated.
It is all the same to me
Where I find myself isolated,

Over which stones, quite alone,
I trail my way home with my bazaar bag
To some house that doesn't know it's mine,
A house like a hospital or a barrack.

It's utterly the same to me
Among what faces like a caged-in lion
I bristle, what human company
Excludes me unfailingly to the iron

Shackles of myself, my subjectivity,
Like a polar bear with no floe to sit on.
Where not to get attached (I don't try!)
Where to degrade myself – it's all one.

And I'll not let the milky call
Of my own native language cheat me –
Which I'm not understood in's all
The same to me, and those who meet me.

(That reader, swallowing his ton
Of newsprint, milker of rumours, hearsay.)
It is a twentieth century tongue,
I stand before any age or century.

Dumbfounded, like the stump of a tree,
The last one left the length of the alley,
All are equal to me, all's the same to me,
And perhaps most of all the same, finally,

Is everything from my native past.
Each mark I've made, my every feature
That past's hand has wiped clean, erased:
Even my soul that was born – somewhere.

So it is my country couldn't keep
Me and the most clever, keenest detective,
Studying my soul, however deep,
Won't find it out – my hidden birthmark.

Each house, each shrine is strange to me,
All is the same, and all is one.
But if along the road I see
A tree, especially a rowan…

[1934]

Elder

The elder has sluiced the yard clean.
The elder is green, it is green.
Greener than mould in a barrel.
Means beginning of summer's apparel.
Till the end of our days: blue skies.
The elder – greener than my eyes.

But then, like Moscow ablaze,
Overnight in our eyes a red haze
From the elder's bubbling and trilling.
Redder than measle-spots filling
My body, in all the air's pores
The multiplying scars

Of the elder.
                    Don't ring, don't ring!
What colours those were, clustering
Sweeter than poison, in berries.
Blend of calico, sealing-wax, Hades.
Gleam of fine coral beads, the taste
Of blood that has dried to a paste.

The elder's been executed.
The elder has sluiced the yard red
With the blood of the young and the innocent,
Blood of twigs' wrists, fire-radiant –
Of all bloods, the most full of fun:
The blood of your heart and my own.

But then came the grain's waterfall.
And then the elder was all
Black with a plum-sticky clinging.
Like a violin, a gate was singing,
Wailing near a house that stood bare, –
One solitary elder grew there.

New settlers in my land!
Because of those berries and
The crimson thirst of my childhood,
Because of the tree and that one word
"Elder" (to this day – at night...)
That poison sucked in by my sight...

[11 September 1931 – 21 May 1935]

My window

My window is very high.
You won't reach it with your finger.
Like a cross on my attic wall
The sun has come to linger.

The window frame's delicate cross.
Peace. – For all eternity.
And I fancy it's as if I was
Being buried in the sky.

[End of November 1919]

I used to write it out on schoolroom slates
(to S.E.)

I used to write it out on schoolroom slates
And on the folds of fans that had grown faded,
On sea and river sand, on ice with skates,
And with my ring on windows I'd engrave it, –

On trunks of trees, a hundred winters old,
Over again: I love you, love you, love you,
And finally, so everyone was told,
I'd register our marriage with a rainbow.

How I wished that with me each would flower up
For centuries! Beneath my fingertips!
And how then, forehead bowing on table top,
I'd cross his name out with a crucifix.

But you, clutched by a scribe for sale, suffering
That grip! Why do you wound my heart with sadness?
Unsold by me! *Inside* the ring!
You will come out unscathed upon these tablets.

[18 May 1920]

Poems grow

Poems grow in the same way as stars and roses,
Or beauty unwished by a family.
To all the wreaths and apotheoses
One answer: – from where has this come to me?

We sleep, and suddenly, moving through flagstones,
The celestial, four-petalled guest appears.
O world, grasp this! By the singer – in sleep – are opened
The stars' law, and the formula of the flowers.

[14 August 1918]

My day

My day is dissipated, mad.
I ask the beggar to give bread,
I give the rich man pauper's pennies.

With light I thread my needle's eye,
I give the burglar my door's key,
With white I rouge my face's paleness.

The beggar will not give a thing,
The rich man spurns my offering,
The light will not go through the needle.

The thief gets in without the key,
The idiot woman weeps her three
Streams over a day absurd, ignoble.

[29 July 1918]

There are happy men and women

There are happy men and women
Who *can't* sing. Well, they must
Shed tears! How sweet it is for them
To pour their grief out in a cloudburst!

So that under the stone there stirs something.
But my calling is like a whip's sting –
Amidst all the funeral's sobbing
Duty commands – to sing.

Though his friend clove in two as he fell,
With his singing King David continued.
If Orpheus had not gone to hell,
But his voice, instead, had descended

Alone there in the dark wood,
While he himself stood on the threshold,
Superfluous – Eurydice would
Have come out on it as on a tightrope.

As on a tightrope and as to light's joys,
Blind, beyond going back, and unshaken.
For, poet, once you're given a voice,
From you all else is taken.

[January 1935]

You, who loved me

You, who loved me with the deceptions
Of truth – and the truth of lies,
You, who loved me – beyond all distance!
– Beyond boundaries!

You, who loved me further
Than time – your hands soared like birds! –
You don't love me any longer:
That's the truth in six words.

[12 December 1923]

Garden

Cure for this hell,
This fever, send
Me a garden down
Toward my life's end,

Toward my life's end,
For my life's cares,
My years of work,
My hunchbacked years...

Toward my life's end,
Dog-like – a bone,
Of burning years –
Cool garden stone.

For an outcast, send
A garden down,
With no one in,
No one around.

Garden: not a step!
Garden: not an eye!
Garden: not a peep!
Garden: not a cry!

Send me a garden down,
Deaf to every call,
With no sweetheart,
No hearts at all.

Tell me: 'Of sorrow, that's enough –
Have a garden – lonely as yourself.'
(Only Yourself don't stand nearby!)
'A garden as solitary as I.'

That's the garden I want, when I grow old...
That garden? Maybe – that future world?
For my old age send it to me,
To take my soul and set it free.

[1 October 1934]

I'm a sheet of paper for your pen

I'm a sheet of paper for your pen.
I will take all. I am a page of whiteness.
Over all your goods, I'm guardian –
I'll give it back with hundred-figured increase.

The country, black and fertile earth, I lie.
You to me are the sun and the rain's vapour.
You are Lord and you are Master. I,
Am this black earth, this white expanse of paper.

[10 July 1918]

I thank you, Lord

I thank you, Lord,
For the Land and the Ocean.
For flesh adored,
For the soul's duration,

Hot blood, cold water,
All of these, together.
– I thank you for love.
I thank you for the weather.

[9 November 1918]

I've opened my veins

I've opened my veins: unstoppably,
Irrestorably, life spurts in sheets.
Bring your basins, bring your plates.
Every plate will be too small.
Every basin too shallow.
                    Over the brim – *past* it –
To the black earth, to nourish the reeds.
Irrevocably, unstoppably,
Irrestorably, verse spurts in sheets.

[6 January 1934]

Poem of the End

1

Pillar in a sky more rusted
Than tin-plate.
He rose in the place appointed
Like fate.

'Quarter to. Am I punctual?' –
'Death doesn't wait.'
Much too smooth and gentle
The rise of his hat.

Challenge in every eyelash.
Clamped shut, his mouth.
Exaggeratedly obsequious
The way he bowed.

'Quarter to? Am I on time?'
His voice lying again.
My heart sank. What's wrong?
Signal in my brain.

Sky of evil portents:
Tin and rust.
He stood at the usual crossroads.
Time: six o'clock, just.

This kiss is a soundless kiss:
Lips stupefied.
As one kisses the hand of empress,
Or a dead man's eyes.

Scurrying street crowds jostle,
Elbow-impaling:
Somewhere a factory whistle,
Exaggeratedly wailing.

Wailing, like some mongrel's howling,
Long, full of wrath.
(Exaggeratedness of life, falling
At the hour of death.)

What was yesterday waist high
Now touches the stars.
(Exaggerated, that means, really,
Grown to full force.)

Mentally: sweetheart, sweetheart.
'It's seven, the time.
Shall we go to the pictures or...'
Explosion: 'Home!'

2

A brethren of nomads, –
To that we have grown.
Thunder on our bare heads,
Our sabres drawn,

With all the terrors filling
Words we wait to come,
Like a home toppling
The word: home.

'Home!' the brat's
Prodigal whine.
And the year-old infant's
'Gimme! Mine!'

My brother in waywardness,
My chill, my heat,
The way you go home
Other people rush out.

Like a horse losing its tethering –
Up! – and the rope's snapped through.
'But there's no home, you know, anywhere!'
'Yes, there is, ten paces from you:

A home on a mountain.' 'Not higher?'
'A home on a mountain top.
Right under the roof there's a window.'
'*One that burns, flaring up*

Not with dawn alone? Must I live it twice,
My life? Simplicity of the poem!
A home, that means out of one's home
Into the night.
                    (O, to whom

Shall I sing my sorrow, my trouble,
Horror that's greener than ice?..)'
'You've been thinking too much, that's all.'
A slow and worried: 'Yes.'

3

And – the embankment. Still I embrace
The water like a solid thickness.
The gardens of Semiramis,
The hanging ones: your likeness.

I hug the water's steely bar,
The colour of corpses, ashen,
Like singers hugging a music score
Or blind men grasping

A railing?..Won't you give back? Not if I first
Kneel down? Can you hear me?
I clutch the assuageress of all thirst
As rain-gutters are clutched, sheerly,

By lunatics…
                No river spawned
This chill – I was born a Naïad!
To clutch the river like the hand
When one's lover is beside

One, and faithful…They're faithful, the dead.
Yes, but we can't all lie in boxes…
Death's on my left. On my right side,
You. My right side is like a corpse's.

A burst of astounding light stands still.
A laugh like a cheap tambourine.
'You and I we ought to…
                (Chill.)
Are we going to behave like men?'

4

A blond-haired mist, a wave of fog,
A flounce of gassy, gauzy stuff,
A lot of breath, a lot of smoke,
But more than that, talk, talk enough.
And what's that smell? Of hurrying,
Indulgences and sins,
Of business secrets scurrying
And powder for the dance.

The family men like bachelors
In rings, such boys, so venerable…
A lot of jokes, a lot of laughs,
But counting's what comes first of all!
The big shots and the little shots,
The ones involved in shabby plans
…The shady deals, the trade secrets,
And powder for the dance.

(Half turned-away: – But can *this* be
Our home? – I'm not the mistress here.)
One sits, his cheque book on his knee,
One holds a dress glove very near,
And this one labours silently
At a dainty shoe that shines.
The business secrets, marriages,
And powder for the dance.

In the window's a silvery notch –
The Maltese Cross is what it is.
Caress a lot and love a lot,
But best of all some squeeze and press
And pinch…(The food is yesterday's.
Forgive its gamy scents.)
The business tricks and escapades,
And powder for the dance.

The chain's a little short, perhaps?
And it's not steel, it's platinum.
With treble chins, shaking their chops,
The cows munch cutlets placidly,
And chew…Above a sugary neck
The devil like a gas-lamp burns,
…The business slumps, the ruin and wrack,
And powder that's someone's –

Berthold Schwartz's…
A clever
Man – to one and all, a friend.
'You and I, we ought to talk together.
Are we going to behave like men?'

5

I watch the way his lips move
And I know he'll not be first to say it.
'You don't love me.' 'Yes, I do.'
'You don't love me.' 'But I'm tormented,

Sucked dry, all my energy's gone
(Like an eagle surveying a locality):
Forgive me, but is this really *home*?'
'My home's in my heart.' 'It's in literature!'

'Love, love is flesh and blood.
Flower, to water which its own blood is able.
Do you really suppose that love
Is conversing across a table?

An hour or two – then home by nine?
Like those gentlemen and ladies?
Love, it means...'
'A shrine?'
– My child, in the shrine's place

Put scar upon scar. 'Under servants' eyes,
Under revellers?' (I, without making
The words heard: Love, it signifies
A bow, stretched: a bow: breaking.)

'Love, it means a liaison.
All's unlinked with us: mouths, existences.'
(I implored you: Don't condemn us,
At that hour of sacred closeness,

That hour at the mountain's top,
At our passion's. Memento – dissolving.
Love, it means to drop
All one's gifts in the fire – for nothing.)

His mouth's shell-like orifice
Is pale. Not a smile – an inventory.
'And more than anything else
One bed.'
'You meant to say

Abyss?' – Drumbeat, in time
Of fingers. 'It'll move no mountains.
Love, it means...' – 'Mine.
I understand you. Conclusion?'

The drumbeat of fingers, tapped
Louder. (Scaffold, drill-square.)
'Let's leave.' – 'And I had hoped
For "let's die" – it's easier!

Enough of this vulgar strife:
These rhymes, rails, hotel rooms, stations...'
'Love, it means: life.' –
'It was named otherwise by the ancients...'

'And so?'
(A corner
Of stray
Handkerchief in a fist, like a fish.)
'Shall we go?' 'What's the itinerary?'
Prisons, bullets, rails – you choose which!

Death – and no prior plans.
'Life!' – Like a Roman general,
Eagle-like, surveying the last strands
Of his men.
'Then let's say farewell.'

6

'I did not want this at all.
Not this. (Silently: listen,
To want is the body's role,
But from this day we're spirits

For each other...) Nor did I say this.
(At the train's departure hour
You give to women, like a cup,
The sad and privileged honour

Of being the one to leave...) Delirium, maybe?
Did I hear wrong? (The liar politely
Gives his lover, like a bouquet,
The bloody honour, lightly,

Of making the break...Each syllable's clear
And so let's say farewell, then.
Did you say it? (Like a handkerchief's square
In the hour of sweet outrage, oblivion,

Dropped...) Of this battle you
Are Caesar.' (O thrust of insolence!
Like a trophy you render to
Your opponent the sword of his own demise!)

He continues. (There's a ringing in my ears).
'I bow twice, I make my obeisances.
For the first time I'm last, it appears,
To break.' 'Do you do this to all the girls?

Don't deny it. It's a vengeance
Worthy of a Lovelace.
An honourable gesture
Which for me divorces

Flesh from bone.' A laugh. Through death,
Laughter. A gesture (No, desire,
Wanting is what gives *those* people flesh,
But we, from this day forward, are

Shadows...) The last nail is pressed
In, hammered. A screw, for the coffin
Is of lead. 'I have one last request.'
'Go ahead.' 'Not one word, even,

About us...not one word, not anything,
To those after me' (so, from their stretchers
The wounded look forward to spring.)
'That's just what I, too, would have requested.

Should I give you a keepsake, to recall?'
'No.' Your gaze, always open, revealed,
Is missing. (Like a seal
Upon thine heart, like a seal

Upon thine arm...No scenes, none.
I swallow it.) More stealthy and silent:

'But a book then?' 'As you'd give anyone?
No, and you'd do better not to write them

At all, books...'

So there's no need.
So there's no need.
No need for crying.

In our wandering
Fishermen's brotherhood
They're dancing, not crying.

They're drinking, not crying,
With hot blood buying
Their lives, not crying.

They are floating
Their pearls in their glasses.
Mustering, not crying.

To go, must I be the one?
I see: Harlequin, for fidelity,
Tossing Pierrette, like a bone,
The meanest, most wretched priority:

The honour of the end.
The curtain's gesture. The concluding
Speech. An inch of lead sent
Into my heart would be better, more scalding

And – cleaner... Grip
Of teeth on lip.
I will not cry.

Uttermost fortress –
On utmost flesh-softness,
Just to keep from crying.

In those wandering brotherhoods
They die but do no crying,
Burn but do no crying.

In ashes and singing
They hide their dead and dying
In these wandering brotherhoods.

I'm first then? It's my first move?
Like chess, you mean? Incidentally,
We are even the first to be shoved
Up to the scaffold...
'Make it snappy,

Please, and don't look!' A look.
(Already they're firing the volley.
But how to turn them back
Into my eyes?) 'I say, categorically,

Don't look!!!'

My loudest and clearest,
My eyes in the sky:
'Let's get going, dearest,
I'm starting to cry.'

I'd forgotten. Among these living
Moneybags (and businessmen)
A blond-haired nape glistened:
Rye, maize and corn!

Effacing all the commandments of Sinai,
Maenads in furs,
Golconda of hair, shining
Custodian of delights –

(for all!) Nature doesn't make savings
For nothing, isn't thrifty in vain.
Hunters, out of these blond-haired tropics
Where is the path that was hewn,

That leads back? With nakedness, vulgar,
Teasing to tears, blinding each eye,
Adultery, sheer, gold laughter,
Poured itself into me.

'Is it not so?' – A look, clinging pensively.
In every eyelash an itch.
But mostly it was the density,
Gesture, plaiting hair to a twist.

O gesture, tending our garments,
Simpler than to eat or to drink –
Wry smile! (For you, alas, there is
Hope of salvation, I think.)

And – was it sisterly, brotherly?
Affair-like: an affair, sure enough!
To laugh, without having buried,
(And, having buried, I laugh.)

7

And – the embankment. The last one.
That's all. Apart, not touching hands,
We wander, like neighbours
Shunning each other. From the river descends –

A sobbing. Without care I lick falling
Mercury. It tastes salt.
For my tears no huge moon of Solomon
Is sent by the heavens' vault.

A post. My forehead, why not batter
It to blood? Or shatter it – but no blood!
Like two accomplices ajitter
We wander (what's murdered is – love).

Stop that. These can't be two lovers?
Into the night. Apart. To another's bed?
'Do you understand that the future's
There?' And I throw back my head.

To sleep. On the rug, like two newly-weds...
To sleep. Still our feet won't fall
In step. Plaintively: – 'Take my arm in yours,
We're not convicts, after all!'

An electric shock. (As if a current
Has passed via my *soul* through my hand.)
A shock, leaping crazy circuits.
On my soul his hand comes to land.

It sticks. Rainbows. What has more rainbows
Than tears? Thicker than beads, curtain-swell
Of rain. 'I don't know of such embankments,
That end.' A bridge – and
'Well?'

Here? (The hearse waits in readiness.)
Tran-quil the climb
Of your eyes. 'May I see you home?
For the last time!'

8

The fi-nal bridge.
(I won't let his arm go, surrender it.)
The fi-nal bridge.
The last, the final girder.

Wa-ter and earth.
I lay the coins out neatly.
Mo-ney for death,
Charon's reward for Lethe.

Sha-dow of coins
In a hand of shadows. Soundless
Are – those – coins.
And so to a hand of shadows

Sha-dows of coins.
Without tinkle or brilliance.
The coins are for them.
The dead have enough of poppies.

The bridge

Hap-py the lot,
The lot without hope, of lovers:
Bridge, you are like hot
Passion, sheer between, common practice.

I nest. It's warm.
A rib – So I cling, tenacious.
No *to*, no *from*:
Vision of spans and spaces.

Arms, legs are gone.
In every bone and emplacement:
Alive in my side alone,
With which I press someone adjacent.

All my life's in my side.
It's an ear and also an echo.
Like a yoke to a white I stick
I stick, or a Samoyed onto

His fur. I batten there.
Siamese twins, stuck together,
With us you can't compare.
That woman, remember, mother

You called her, how well
Within her she carried you, joyously,
Oblivious and still,
She held you no more closely.

Look! We're used to each other! We're here!
You sang lullabies to me, tender.
I won't throw myself into the weir
Because I would have to surrender

Your hand. I press and
I press even harder, can't be severed.
Bridge, you're no married man:

Sheer

Your hand. I press and
I press even harder, can't be severed.
Bridge, you're no married man:
You're sheer *en passant*: you're a lover.

Bridge – you're for us, our support.
We feed the river with our bodies.
Like ivy I've bored,
Like a tick. Tear me out by my root-tips.

A tick, burrowing.
Godless and base, inhuman.
Throw me away like a thing,
Me who have no even

One thing I esteemed
In all this void, thing-laden cosmos.
Tell me it's something I dreamed.
That it's night, and that day follows,

An ex-press, and Rome.
Granada. Even I have no idea,
Having cast off feather beds like some
Montblancs or Himalayas.

It's deep this glade:
I warm it with the last blood of my body.
Feel my side.
After all, at least it's more steady

Than verses... Warm through
Now? Who'll you be kissing tomorrow night?
Tell me it's not true,
That the bridge is, will always be without

Its end...

– End.

'Here?' A childlike, godlike
Gesture. 'Well?' Battened in, fast...
'A little while longer:
For this time, for the last!'

Like factory buildings, stentorian
And responsive to a call...
Sublingual and best hidden
Secret of wives from all

Husbands, of widows from those they know:
Cherished secret Eve took from the tree with her:
I am nothing more than an animal
Wounded in the anima.

Burning pain: like my soul being torn away
With my skin. Like steam through a hole,
It has left, notorious, worthless heresy
That carries the name of soul.

Christian chlorosis.
Steam. What help can poultices give!
It never even existed.
A body was, wanted to live.

Now does not want to.

– Forgive me, I didn't mean it!
The sob of those whipped inside out.
Thus at four o'clock in the morning
Condemned men wait to be shot,

With a smile, ironic, teasing
The corridor's Judas, at chess.
It's true: we are pawns in a chess-game,
And someone is playing at us.

Who? Thieves? The gods in heaven?
The peephole is filled by an eye.
The clank of the red corridor.
The board is lifted away.

A drag on the coarse tobacco.
Spit. – They've had it, then. Spit.
Over this paving is chequered
A straight road to the pit

And the blood. The eye, secret:
The dormer eye of the moon…
………………………………
And, straining, squinting, sidetracked:
'How far you've already gone!'

10

A combined and united
Shiver. – Our milkbar!

Our island, our shrine
Where in morning time

– Riff-raff! Couple for minutes! –
We'd celebrate matins.

Smell of rust, a bazaar-smell
Of spring and dreams' fluff…

The coffee here was pigswill, –
Oats, terrible stuff!

(Oats can disable
A trotter's verve!)
It smelt quite un-Arabian –
Arcadian was the whiff

Of that coffee…

But how she would smile to us,
Sit down with us awhile,
Worldly-wise, dolorous, –
With her solicitous smile

Of a grey-haired paramour:
– You'll fade! Better live!
With madness and poverty
For yawning and love –

But mainly for youthfulness,
Mirth without cause,
For smiling innocence,
Faces without flaws –

Yes, mainly for youthfulness.
For passions ill-climated,
Blown in from some other source,
Swept in from some other shores

To this milkbar's darkness:
– Tunis and burnous! –
For hopes and muscles
Under shabby clothes.

(Dearest, I'm not complaining.
Just scar on scar.) Much
Did she like chaperoning
Us out, her cap Dutch,

So stiff-ironed, our hostess…

Not remembering, nor quite comprehending,
As from some feast we are led away…
– Our street. – But it's not ours, already.
– So many times… – No more shall we…

– In the west the sunrise will be waiting.
– And David will break with the Lord.
– What is it we're doing? – Separating.
– I don't understand that word,

Word that is supersenseless.
'Sep-arating.' Of hundreds I'm separate?
Just a word with four syllables,
Behind which there's an empty spot.

Is it true in Serbian, Croatian?
Maybe it's some Czech fantasy?
Separating. Sep-aration…
Supernatural absurdity!

A sound that makes ears burst, pushing
Them to the outer reaches of pain…
Separation – it just isn't Russian.
It's not language of women! Of men!

Nor of God! Are we sheep, dully viewing
Our food, as we yawn and make do?
Separation, what language are you in,
When there's no meaning to be found for you?

Not even a sound. Just a hollow
Rasp, like a saw, say, through sleep.
Separation is simply the Khlebnikov
School's nightingales that weep

Like swans…
                    But how has it happened?
Like a reservoir running dry –
The air! I can feel hands touching.
Separation's a bolt from the sky.

On our heads... Sea flooding the cabin!
Oceania's furthest cape.
These streets are far too sloping:
Separation's a downward leap,

Down the mountain... Sigh of two heavy
Bootsoles... Last, a palm, and a nail in place.
A conclusion more sweeping than any.
Separated – that means separate ways,

Yet we'd grown as one...

11

All at once to lose all –
No purer way.
Suburb, last port of call:
End of our days.

End to our joys (read millstones),
To days and houses and us.

Empty dachas! I have revered
You as might an aged mother.
It's hard work, after all, being empty there,
Being empty's not like being hollow.

(Dachas, a third of you empty and bare,
You'd do better to burn, and not be there!)

Only don't tremble
Faced with your open wound's lip.
To the suburbs, the suburbs,
Seams that rip.

For, not to dream up a stream
Of long words: love is a seam.

A seam, not a sling. A seam, not a shield
– O don't ask to be shielded! –

The seam that sews the dead to the earth
Is the one by which I'm sewn to you.

(Time will tell, by what kind of stitch,
Plain or treble, which!)

One way or another, my friend – burst seams!
Shreds, rags and tatters!
Only what bursts is worth any esteem
– Bursts, hasn't merely unravelled.

Where under the basting-thread a live vein's
Redness shows, not decayed remains.

O those who burst and tear
Know no loss.
Suburb, outer sphere:
Foreheads' divorce.

The execution's today,
In the suburbs a draught to our brains!

They know no less, those who are gone
In the hour when the dawn is breaking.
I have sewed your life for you all night long,
For good, without any basting.

So don't reproach me that it's off beam:
Suburb: bursting of seams!

Souls that are unprepared
Are covered in tears...
Outer sphere, suburb...
Abyss of arms,

Of the suburb. Like destiny's tread,
Can you hear it – on clay turned to liquid?
...Judge this tenacious thread,
My friend, my hand's careless, hurried

Motion – however long it may take.
The final lamp post.

'Here?' Like a conspiracy,
A look. Of those trodden down.
'Can we climb the mountain?'
For the last time, we can.

12

Like a thick horse's mane,
Rain in eyes. And hills.
We're in the suburbs again,
We've left the city walls.

Stepmothers aren't mothers
With generous stock,
Not for us – there's nowhere
For us, here we must croak.

We're brother and sister.
A field. And a fence.
Life is a suburb.
Out of town, build your house.

Ladies and gentlemen,
It's a hopeless affair.
The suburbs are legion,
The cities are – where?

The rain beats and rages.
We stand, breaking. Adieu.
After three months, three ages,
Our first time as two.

Wasn't it Job, God,
You asked for a loan?
The venture's miscarried:
We're out of town.

Out of town! Understand? Out! You must move
Beyond! You've crossed on your own!
Life is the place where no one may live:
It's the Jewish zone.

So isn't it a hundredfold more erect
To become an eternal Jew?
Since for everyone who's not wholly a shit
Life is equal to

A pogrom of Jews! Life's for converts,
The Judases of faith.
Go to hell, the penal islands, anywhere,
But not to life,

That spares only the traitor, the lamb
For the executioner's knife.
On this document I stamp,
On my ticket for life.

I crush it. In vengeance for David's shield.
Into the mangled bodies' mess.
It's intoxicating that a Jew refused life,
That he didn't say yes?

Expect no mercy. The ghetto enfolds
The chosen few.
In this most Christian of all worlds
The poet's a Jew.

13

Thus one sharpens knives on a whetstone,
Thus with brooms one sweeps away
Sawdust. The palms of hands rest on
Something wet and furry.

Where are you, twins, doubles:
Power and dryness of men?
Under my hands' palms –
Tears, not rain!

What other temptations
To speak of? What's mine turns to water!
After your eyes like diamonds
Flow through my hands with their glitter,

I have nothing to lose.
To lose. The end's in place.
I am stroking, stroking,
Stroking your face.

That's the sort of pride we Marinkas
Have, after all, we are Polish girls.
After your eyes, an eagle's,
Sobbing beneath my palm's caress...

You're crying? My dearest.
Forgive me – my all.
In my palm, how luxuriant
The salt tears fall.

Men's tears are tears of cruelty:
A club blow to the temple.
The shame that you have lost on me
You'll make up with others amply.

We are fishes swimming
In the same sea. A lift:
...Like the dead seashell
Of a lip on lips.

In tears.
Goose-foot –
To the taste.
– And tomorrow
When I'm awake?
Awake?

14

Descent. Along a sheep path.
The city blares.
Three whores come toward us,
They're laughing. At tears,

Like a deep sea-wind, southerly,
Like the crests of waves,
Laughing scorn at the manly,
The needless disgrace

Of your tears which are obvious
Through the rain two scars away,
Like pearls set, inglorious,
In a warrior's bronze array,

At your tears, first and last ones,
Oh – let them pour down.
At your tears which are ornaments,
Pearls for my crown!

I don't let my eyes fall,
Through the rain I stare.
Stare, Venus's dolls,
For this affair

Brings much closer
Than going to bed!
The Song of Songs, even,
Gives us the word,

Even Solomon begs us,
Birds of low esteem,
– Our consorted sobbing
Is more than sleep or dream.

And into the hollow waves
Of the murk, even, hunched up –
With no trace – with no murmur,
Like a sinking ship.

[Prague, 1 December 1924 – Ilovišći, 8 June 1924]

Poems to Czechia

1

The land is full and free.
Only one thing causes cares:
The Czechs don't have a sea.
Their sea's a sea of tears.

Salt they don't need at all,
They've stocks for years in store.
Three hundred years of thrall,
Of liberty, one score.

Freedom, of God, of men,
Not useless, as of birds.
Greatnesses's years: twice ten,
Twice ten of Czech dialect words

On the calm field, for all,
Of *one* people, not more.
Three hundred years of thrall,
Of liberty, one score.

For all. A hearth, a home.
For all. Games, learning and
Work for all who come
And can lend a hand.

In every field and school
Watch the new shoots soar.
Three hundred years of thrall,
Of liberty, one score.

Come, guests of the Czech land,
Confirm in unison:
What's sown with a full hand
With honour's built and won.

For two decades' rebirth
(And even that cut short)
As nowhere else on earth
Songs were sung, thoughts thought.

Vltava's waves groan, call,
Turned grey from suffering sore:
'Three hundred years of thrall,
Of liberty, one score.'

On eagle rocks hunched to,
Like an eagle with its prey –
What have they done to you,
My realm, my Czech country?

Your mountains made to fall,
Your streams made not to pour.
Three hundred years of thrall,
Of liberty, one score.

In every village for miles
Joy's woven, red and blue.
Czech lion with two tails,
What have they done to you?

The foxes have made small
The forest's commodore.
Three hundred years of thrall,
Of liberty, one score.

Listen with every tree,
Forest, and know, Vltava.
Wrath, lion* rhyme for me:
Vltava rhymes with *slava*.

An hour or two is all
Your span of misery.
Through the night of thrall
Shines white day of liberty.

[12 November 1938]

NOTE **In Russian* lev *is 'lion', and* gnev *'wrath', 'anger'* – D.McD.

2

Reserved for aurochs, mountainsides.
Black, the forests lie.
Valleys look into the rivers,
Mountains look into the sky.

Most free of any region,
More generous, there's none.
These mountains: native country
Of my child, my son.

Valleys, four does, a pasture.
Not to disturb the beasts,
The huts hide under rafters,
And in wooded retreats

For miles, however many,
There's not one single gun.
These valleys: native country
Of my child, my son.

There I raised my son, my child.
What flowed? Water? Days?
Or was it the white flocks
Of geese across the skies?

The currant bushes are celebrating
Nativity of summer and sun.
These huts are the native country
Of my child, my son.

That birth into the world was
A birth into Paradise.
God, when He'd made Bohemia,
Spake: 'This land is glorious,

Has all the gifts that nature gives,
Each and every one,
More generous than the Native Land
Of My Child, My Son.'

The Czechoslovak underlayer:
Marriage of streams and rock.
God, when He'd made Bohemia,
Spake: 'This was a noble work.'

Everything was there, excepting
Orphans – of those there were none,
In the native country
Of my child, my son.

Cursed be who've occupied
That peaceloving realm.
With hares and deer together
With every pheasant's feather.

Thrice cursed be those who sold you out,
They'll never be forgiven.
Everlasting native land
Of those who've none to live in.

My land, my land that has been sold,
Entire, alive, with beasts,
With magic kitchen gardens,
With mountain veins, rock-hardened,

With whole peoples abandoned
On fields without a home,
And sighing: 'My home country,
My native land, my own.'

God's own land. Bohemia.
Don't lie still as a moraine.
God gave to you with both His hands
And He will give again.

In solemn oath they've raised their hands,
All your sons, your children –
They swear to die for the native land
Of those who've none to live in!

[Between 12 and 19 November 1938]

3

The map holds a location:
Look – and blood smears your eyes.
Each hamlet's conflagration
A private Calvary.

Like so many axes
The frontier barriers fall.
The world's flesh has an abscess
That will devour all.

From porch to stately, static
Mountains, to where the eagle rests,
For thousands of quadratic
Irrestorable versts –

An abscess.
                    For a rest
A Czech lay down, was buried alive.
In the nation's breast,
A wound: *our* nation's died.

All they have to say is 'brotherly'
About that land – and there's rain from eyes!
Greed, speculation, celebrate,
You've won a handsome prize.

Greed, for Judas – a libation!
But for us whose hearts still care
The map holds a location
That's void: our honour's there.

[19-22 November 1938]

4 An Officer

In the Sudetenland, on the wooded Czech border, an officer with 20 soldiers, leaving his men in the woods, came out onto the road and began to fire at the approaching Germans. His end is unknown.

From a September newspaper, 1938 – M.Ts.

The essence of forests,
Czech forestry estate.
The year: nineteen hundred
And thirty-eight.

Day and month? Like an echo, the mountains:
'The day the Czechs fell to the Germans.'

The wood's almost red.
The sky, grey-blue, clear.
Twenty soldiers are led
By one officer.

Apple-faced, his forehead sheer,
One officer's guarding his frontier.

My woods, all around.
My shrubs, all around.
My home, all around.
This is my home.

Not one tree will I give up.
Not one house will I give up.
Not one shire will I give up.
Not one *inch* will I give up.

Leaves dark overhead.
In the heart, fright.
The Prussians' tread?
Or my own heartbeat?

My woods, farewell.
My age, farewell.
My land, farewell.
This land is mine.

Let the whole land fall
To the enemy's boot.
I'll give nothing at all,
Not a stone underfoot.

The trampling of feet.
'The Germans': one leaf.
And an iron flood.
'The Germans': the wood.

'The Germans': peal cleft
Into mountain and plain.
One officer's left
All of his men.

From the wood – in lively manner –
Against the behemoth – with a revolver.

A shot resounds.
The whole wood sounds.
Wood: clapping of hands.
All: clapping of hands.

While he lashes the German with lead,
The whole wood applauds overhead.

Maple and pine,
Needles and leaves,
The whole wood's entwined,
Dense, thicketed sheaves –

By all of them
The good news is waved,
The message that's come –
Czech honour is saved.

That means that our
Land is not betrayed.
It means that war
Has been, was made.

Long live my land.
Bite the dust, Herr.
Twenty men and
One officer.

[October 1938 – 17 April 1939]

An Attempt at a Room

The walls of inertia have been counted before me.
But what about chance? A brainstorm?
Of these walls, I've memorised three –
For the fourth, I will not answer.

Who can tell, with one's back to the wall?
Maybe it's there, but maybe not at all

There. It wasn't. Draughty. But no
Wall that's behind your back, then? All that's
Not your wish: the cable, *Dno*:
'Tsar abdicated.' Not only from the post office,

The news. The urgent telegrams race
From every time and every place.

Were you playing the piano? A wind's blown in.
A draught. Moves like a sail. Like cotton-
Wool, fingers. The sonatina's page is turned down
(You're only nine, have you forgotten?).

For the wall that can't be seen
I know a name: wall of the spine

At a piano. Or else – at a desk.
Or yet again – at the business of shaving.
The wall has a way with one of its tricks:
Becoming a corridor, reflected, receding

In the mirror. One look – you're transported there.
Emptiness's metaphorical chair.

A chair for all who won't get through
The door – the threshold's sensitive to bootsoles!
That wall, the one from which you grew –
I've speeded up the past on purpose –

Between us there's still a whole paragraph's
Space. You'll rise up like D'Anzace –

From behind.
For that wall, like D'Anzace, called
And chosen, for fate's hour, majestic
(I know a name for it: wall
Of the *backbone*!) comes in, not at all D'Anthès-like.

The back of the head. Are you ready, then?
Like you after ten stanzas or ten

Lines.
In the nape, an optical attack.
But, leaving aside the behind-back grouping,
The ceiling *was*, there's no mistake.
I won't insist: perhaps slightly stooping,

Squinting at the parlour floor
(A bayonet attack in the rear

Of one's forces).
And now the cerebellum's
Clenched. Like a clod, the back has slumped.
That solid wall under the Cheka's direction,
That wall of dawns, of executions

That are bright: clearer than in the shadow
Of gestures – in the back and from behind it.

What I won't understand. The execution.
But, leaving aside the behind-wall grouping,
The ceiling was demonstrably overhead,
And whole (but let's move on – why dwell on

It?) I return to the fourth wall, toward
Which, in his flight, the coward
Retreats.
'Well, was there a floor,
Then? I mean, it has to be done on something?...'
There was. – Not for all. – Onto a swing,
A tree, a horse, a tightrope, a sabbath,

Higher!...
All of us, in the other world,
Must fuse our heels, here gravity-mired,
With emptiness.

A floor is for feet.
How rooted man is, how embedded.
So that the ceiling doesn't leak.
Remember the ancient torture – one droplet

Per hour? A floor: to stop grass growing into the house,
To stop the earth coming into the house –

With all – those – for whom a picket at the door,
Even, is no obstacle on a May night!
Three walls, a ceiling and a floor.
That's all, it would seem! Now, come into sight!

Will he announce himself with the knock of a shutter?
The room is thrown together in haste,
With whitish tints on grey, a scatter,
A rough draft, merely, traced and sketched.

No roofer, no plasterer –
A dream. On paths with no barbed wire,
A guard. In the abysses under the eyelids
A certain *he* meets a certain *her*.

No provisioner, no furnisher –
A dream. More naked, bare
Than the Reval sandbank. Floor without varnishes,
A room? Rather – just – surfaces.

A platform's more friendly,
Something from geometry,
Abyss in a textbook,
Late, but quite understood.

But is the brake of phaetons
A table? For, after all, a table is fed
By an elbow. Elbow it according to your inclination
– It'll be a table always ready to hand.

Just like storks announcing babies
If you need it, the thing is there. –
Don't worry before your guest's arrival –
When the guest comes, the chair will appear.

It'll all grow fine.
Don't meddle and fuss.
Shall I tell you what sign
Hangs above its place?

Mutual feelings.
Calm of wooded knolls
Hotel
Rendezvous of Souls.

A meeting house. All – those partings,
Even southward, for southern ones!
Do hands do the service?
No, but something quieter than hands,

And lighter than hands, and purer
Than hands. A renovated byre
With service? The thin, poor
Creatures abandoned there!

Yes, here we are truly
Touch-me-nots. Heralds of hands,
Thoughts of hands, end-results of hands,
Utmost extremities of hands…

Without convulsive 'where-are-you's'
I wait. In closest kinship with silence
Nothing except pure gestures
Serve within Psyche's palace.

To the poet, only the wind is dear.
Of this, only in corridors I am sure.

A march past – that's the armies' base.
It takes a long march so as all at once,
In the room's midst, with the look of a god,
Of a poet, a lyrist
the poem's road!

Wind, wind, like a banner above foreheads,
Raised aloft as we march forwards!

An institutionalised 'so on to infinity' –
Corridor's: distance's domesticity.

With my corvine profile of a heterodox woman,
Distance, with quiet speed, to the rhythm

Of children's feet, in my raincoat's rustle
The dear rhymes: *grifel', tufel'* –

Kafel'...in a peacock train's shuffle
Somewhere the tower that is called Eiffel.

As a river for a child's just a pebble in motion
So distance isn't distance, just an orange section.

In the child's stringed, grounded memories,
Distance with hand baggage, distance – governess...

Not deigning to tell us (distance in fashions)
What's being hauled on those carts in the traffic...

Distance reduced to a pencil case...
Corridors: canals inside houses.

Fates, events, dates, wedding days –
Corridors: tributaries inside houses.

With anonymous letters at five in the morning,
Along the corridor walk not only

Brooms. Smell of thyme and turf, alloyed.
Occupation? Corridor boy!

My duties demanding, and that's all,
That in corridors I grind out – the Carmagnole!

Whoever's been involved in the construction
Of corridors knows the right direction

In which to bend to give the blood time
To tie itself round the heart's corner, to twine

Itself round that corner, that angle
Acute, of thunderbolts the magnet!
So that the island of the heart
Should be washed in every part.

This corridor is created by me.
Don't ask for further clarity.
In order to give the train time
To give warning along the whole line:

From 'passengers not taken on'
As far as the heart's farthest junction:
'The train's leaving! Throw yourself on the track,
And if not – then get off it, and stand back.'

This corridor's created be me –
I'm not a poet – unreflectingly!
In order to give the brain time
To allot places, to set, align,

For a rendezvous is a locality,
A list – calculation, sketch –
Of words that are not always apposite,
Of gestures all wrong, simply out of touch.

So that love may be in order –
That all of it may be dear to you –
All, to the very last fold
Of lips, of dress? Of brow.

They all know how to smooth out a dress!
Corridors: tunnels inside houses.

Like the old man whom his daughter shepherds.
Corridors: ravines inside houses.

Look, friend: as in a letter or dream
I bring this ray of hope to you, one gleam!

In the first sleep when you lower your eyelids
I bring this to you as a foretaste

Of light. At time's most extreme point
This is I – an eye of light.

What happens then?
The dream is: right.
There was a rise,
A downward flight

Of brow – with brow.
Your brow's going forth,
In front: the rhyme's
Coarse: a mouth.

Was it because the walls had disappeared –
The ceiling demonstrably keeled

Over. Only the vocative flowered in each
Mouth. But the floor's demonstrably a breach

And through the breach, as green as the Nile…
The ceiling demonstrably started to sail.

While the floor – what's there to say to the floor
But 'collapse!'. What use have we for

Cheap floorboards? Not enough whitewash? Too bad!
The whole of a poet's sustained and held

By one dash…
                    The ceiling's overhang
Above two bodies' nothing demonstrably sang –

Like all the angels.

[St Gilles-sur-Vie, 6 June 1926]

New Year Letter

Happy New Year – light, world, realm, haven – to you,
My first epistle to you in your new
– To call it lush would be miscomprehension –
Lush, ruminant place: clamorous, stentorian
Like the deserted tower of Aeolus.
My first epistle to you from yesterday's
– In which, without you I shall fret and pine –
Homeland, already now, for you, from one
Of heaven's stars... Law of retreat, withdrawal,
By which any woman is left by anyone at all,
And unreal ones by unrealities.
Shall I tell you how I learned of yours?
There was no earthquake, no abyss's yawn.
Someone walked in – not loved, just anyone.
'It's an event that's causing great distress.
In *News* and *Days*. I hope you'll do a piece?'
'Where?' 'In the mountains.' (Window, fronds of firs,
A bedsheet.) 'Don't you read the newspapers?
You'll do one, then?' 'No.' 'But...' I make excuses.
Aloud: 'Too hard.' Inside: 'I'm not a Judas.'
'In a sanatorium.' (A rented paradise).
'When?' 'One, two days ago. My memory's not precise.'
'Will you talk in Alcazar?' 'No, I think not.'
Aloud: 'His family.' Inside: 'All, but Iscariot.'

Happy break of day! (Tomorrow you were born!)
Shall I tell you what I did after I learned...?
Sh. Out of habit my tongue slips and stammers,
I've long since set both life and death in commas,
As being known-to-be empty gossip, false.
I did nothing. But then something else,
Something that does with no echo and no shade,
Was done...
Tell then, how was the trip you made?
How was it that the heart tore, yet was not torn
Apart? As if on Orlov trotters borne,
They that have an eagle's speed, *you said*,
Taking breath away? Or else perhaps it sped
More, and more sweetly? There exist no heights,

Descents for anyone who has known flight
On real Russian eagles. We are blood-related
With the beyond. Who's been to Russia's sighted
The next world in this one. Well-oiled transition!
I smile a hidden smirk in the pronunciation
Of 'life' and 'death' – my smile's touched by your own.
I say 'life', 'death' with footnotes added on,
An asterisk (the night I wish were near:
Instead of a cerebral hemisphere –
A stellar one!)
                    My friend, do not forget
The following: if the Russian alphabet
Has pushed the German characters away
It's not because now all's one, as they say,
And dead men (beggars) swallow anything,
Don't bat an eyelid! – But because it's plain
– Thirteen, in Novodevichiy, this dawned –
The *next* world isn't tongueless, but all-tongued.

Not without sadness now I ask, implore:
Don't you want to know the Russian for
Nest? The only rhyme for all nests (*gnyozdy*)
Is one that covers all of them: stars (*zyvozdy*).

Did I stray from the point?
                                        That can't be true.
There's no such thing as one that strays from you.
Du Lieber, every syllable and thought
Leads back to you again, no matter what
The theme (though German's really more my own
Than Russian, Angel-talk's most mine). In the same way
As there's no place you aren't – there is: the grave.
All as it wasn't, as it was – but have
You nothing anywhere about me there?
Your surroundings, Rainer, what your feelings are?
Most urgently, and with an assured force,
Your first impression of the universe
(i.e. impression from the poet in it)
And your last vision of our earthly planet,
That's given but once to you – and as a whole!
Vision not of ashes-poet, body-soul
(To isolate one's to offend them both)

But of you with yourself, of you betrothed
With you – being Zeusian doesn't mean one's better –
In you each Pollux meets up with his Castor,
In you each marble statue meets its grass,
Not separation, not a meeting – this,
A confrontation: a meeting and
First parting.
How did you look at your hand
(And at the trace made on it by the ink)
From all your many (how many, do you think?)
Miles – infinite because beginningless –
Height up above the crystal levelness
Of the Mediterranean – and other saucers.
All as it wasn't, will be, with me also
Placed far beyond the suburbs' outer spheres.
All as it wasn't, all as it appears
– What's that to someone writing letters one
Week extra? And where else should one's eyes turn
As one leans on the theatre loge's edge,
From this – except to that, and from that stage
Except to the longsuffering *this*: all views look down.
I live in Bellevue. It's a little town
Of nests and branches. Looking at my guide:
Bellevue. A fortress with a fine view thrown wide
On Paris – palace of Gallic fantasy –
On Paris – and some places further away...
As you lean forward on your scarlet rim
How quaint to you (who) "probably" must seem,
As you look from your boundlessly high spheres,
All our Bellevues and our Belvederes!

I skip. Inconsequence. Expediency.
The New Year's at the door. With whom shall I
Drink toasts, to what? With what? In the foam's place,
A cotton wad. What for? It strikes – my role in this?
What am I to do in all the din of New Year,
With the internal rhyme of 'Rainer – died there'?
If you, if such an eye's snuffed out, in truth
It means that life's not life and death's not death.
It means it's darkening, when we meet it'll dawn,
No life, no death – new, third phenomenon,
For 'twenty-six (bedding 'twenty-seven in straw),

What bliss to end, for 'seven to start with you!
Across the table that the eye can't glimpse,
Will we drink toasts with quiet resonance
Of glass on glass? No bar-room sort: the chime
Of *I* on *you* which fuse to give a rhyme:
Third, new.
Over the table I look at your cross.
How many places out of town, such space
Out here! To whom do bushes wave their boughs
If not to us? These places specially ours,
Not others'! All the leaves! The needles, too!
Places of yours with me (of you with you).
We could have made a rendezvous there, just
To talk. Not only places! But the months!
And weeks! And rainy suburbs, streets with never
A soul! And mornings! And all this together,
And not struck up by any nightingales!

I'm in a pit, so likely my vision fails.
You see more up there, above, that's probable.
Nothing has worked out for us at all.
So purely and so simply nothingness
To fit with our capacity and size
That there's no need for me to list it. Not
A thing, except – do not expect the out-
Of-line (I can't, in truth, say out-of-time)
And anyway, into what norm, what line
Would it fit? One old refrain we sing:
'Nothing can be made out of no-thing.'
O for something, even shade of shadow play!
Nothing at all: that house, that hour, that day.
Even a prisoner in chains, in death row's grips,
Endowed with memory has: those lips!
Or have we looked too long, hard for a cure?
Of all *that* only *that light* was ours for sure,
As we are only the reflection
Of us – in place of this – *that world* beyond!

In the least built-up outskirt of them all,
Happy new place, Rainer, world, Rainer!
At the far cape of the demonstrable,
Happy new vision, Rainer, hearing, Rainer.

To you all was an obstacle:
Passion, even friend.
Happy new sound, Echo!
Happy new echo, Sound!

How often on the schoolroom chair:
What's beyond the mountains? The rivers, there?
Are they pretty, those landscapes without tourists?
Is it true, then, Rainer – heaven's mountainous,
With thunder? Not just the heaven in widows' prayers,
It's not the only heaven, above it there's
Another? With terraces? The Tatras make it clear
That heaven can't be other than an amphitheatre
(A curtain lowered over someone, too...)
That God's a Baobab, Rainer, is it true,
A *growing* tree? And not a Louis d'Or –
God's not alone – but over him's one more
God?

How's your writing going in your new place?
If you're there, so is verse, in any case.
How's your writing in the good life to come
With no desk for your elbow, for your palm
No brow –

In your usual script, send some lines!
Rainer, are you pleased with those new rhymes?
For – to interpret *rhyme* in its truest sense,
What's death if not a whole new range, expanse
Of rhymes?

Impasse. The language's studied through.
A whole new expanse of new sense, and of new
Assonances.

– Till we meet! Are friends!
I don't know if we'll meet, but our songs will blend.
Happy new world, even for me wrapped in mystery –
Happy whole sea, Rainer, happy whole me.
Scribble ahead a few lines – so we don't miss.
Happy new tracery of sounds, Rainer.
In heaven there's a ladder up it with Gifts...
Happy new hand-position, Rainer!

I cup my glass with my palm, so they can't pour me one,
Above the Rhône – and high above Rarogne,
Above pure and simple parting and
Deliver this to Rainer Maria Rilke's hand.

[Bellevue, 7 February 1927]